AGAINST THE TIDE

Series Editor: MEIC STEPHENS

Against the Tide

**Christianity in Wales on the Threshold
of a New Millennium**

D.P.Davies

First Impression—August 1995

ISBN 1 85902 258 8

Printed in Wales at
Gomer Press, Llandysul, Dyfed

'Swift to its close ebbs out life's little day;
Earth's joys grow dim, its glories pass away;
Change and decay in all around I see.'

The hymn from which these words of Henry Francis Lyte are taken represents more than any other the residual folk religion of the English. 'Abide with me' is to Wembley Stadium what 'Guide me, O Thou Great Jehovah' is to the National Stadium at Cardiff Arms Park. So how does this connect to the folk religion of Wales? Certainly the observer of the religious scene in Wales might be tempted to join the choirs of rugby supporters in asking Jehovah to lead him 'pilgrim through this barren land', but for this observer Lyte's words more accurately reflect the state of Christianity, and the Christian Churches in particular, in Wales as we approach the dawn of the third millennium of the Christian era.

'Change and decay'. The signs are all around us. The Churches today—those that have survived—are very different from the Church I knew as a boy half a century ago. And compared with the state of the Churches at the turn of this twentieth century there has been a sea-change.

In these circumstances it is ironical, to say the least, that the current Secretary of State for Wales (Dr John Redwood) should have chosen to remind the people of Wales as they embarked on their Christmas festivities in 1994 that Wales—apparently more so than Dr Redwood's native England—is a Christian country. Dr Redwood's sweeping and unsubstantiated claim prefaced the issuing of a diktat that religious education in Wales must have a stronger biblical base, since the Bible is the foundation of the kind of Christian morality that society, and the Anglican Church in particular, has, according to Redwood, long since abandoned. One would like to think that Dr Redwood's 'Back to the Bible' call to the nation's schools was motivated by evangelical zeal, but the cynic in me tends to conclude that this is yet another attempt to find a scapegoat for the inexorable rise in crime and the rapid disintegration of social values that Redwood's government seems powerless to arrest and for which many suspect they bear considerable responsibility.

What is astonishing, however, is the hypothesis that Wales is still a Christian country, when all the evidence suggests that Welsh society has entered a post-Christian phase. According to the *Western Mail* of 24 December 1994, for example, the combined weekly attendance at the Church in Wales (Anglican) and the Roman Catholic Church in Wales is no more than 100,000. These Churches anticipated their biggest congregations of the year at Christmas, but even then the combined total was a mere 200,000—some way short of ten per cent of the total population of Wales. Since these two Churches are the strongest Churches (numerically) in Wales by some distance, we can reasonably conclude that even at Christmas, with all its sentimental hype about the baby Jesus, the shepherds, the wise men and the manger, even at Christmas, Christianity—in its institutional form at any rate—is a matter of complete indifference to nine out of ten of the population of this so-called Christian country.

The Protestant Fathers must be turning in their graves, especially so since it is now an established fact that there are more Muslims than Methodists in Wales. A century ago things were very different. Even in my own lifetime I can recall a time—not too long ago—when it could be assumed that Wales, whatever might be true of England, was a Christian country, even if Welsh Christians spent much of their time arguing with one another about what constituted the true faith.

So what went wrong? How are we to explain the quite dramatic decline in the fortunes of the Christian Churches in Wales over the course of the twentieth century? Since what follows is a personal analysis, coloured by all manner of personal prejudice, let me introduce myself and say something of where I come from.

I am a Professor of Theology—an academic theologian, that is —at what used to be seen as one of the strongholds of Anglicanism in Wales—University of Wales, Lampeter, or Saint David's College, Lampeter, as it was originally known. As it happens, I am an Anglican, but this is no longer a necessary condition of my post. Indeed, over the past decade the Department of Theology, whose staff in 1980 was exclusively

Anglican and indeed wholly clerical, has been transformed into a thriving Department of Theology *and* Religious Studies, where all the world's major faiths, as well as the phenomenon of religion in general, are studied alongside Christianity. The staff of the Department reflect this mixture of faiths, with adherents of several different faiths—and indeed of none—working alongside one another in a pluralistic environment that mirrors the society in which we live.

In my youth, and even as a young man, I would not in my wildest dreams have imagined that in my fifties I should be teaching theology in such an environment, and in Lampeter of all places! I was born (just before the outbreak of World War II) and brought up in an Anglican vicarage in an Anglicized part of Wales (between Brecon and Hay-on-Wye). Both my parents, however, were Welsh-speaking (originally from the Gwendraeth valley). Welsh was therefore my first language, though to my shame I later lost it and had to relearn my native tongue as an adult. My father had been ordained into the ministry of the Church in Wales in the immediate aftermath of the Disestablishment campaign. This was hardly a favourable climate for an ecumenical approach to Christian witness in Wales. Confrontation rather than dialogue was the watchword. My mother had been brought up in Welsh Calvinistic Methodism, which like her kinsman Saunders Lewis she abandoned on reaching adulthood—in her case for the comparatively calm waters of Anglicanism. I was brought up to think of Welsh Nonconformity (the Chapel) as a defective form of Christianity, not to be counted as the true Church, based as it was (or so I was led to believe) on emotion and narrow-minded bigotry. These views were further reinforced by my schooling at Christ College, Brecon, where Anglicanism was part of the way of life instilled into us. It was not until I went to University (in England) that I came to know and respect Welsh Nonconformists, as I continued to think of them, and the tradition they represented.

My early years in the Christian ministry (of the Church in Wales) and as a teacher of theology at Lampeter were informed by ecumenical idealism. By the 1960s I was convinced that the only way forward for the Churches in Wales was to unite, if not

7

immediately in a single organic union, at least in every conceivable practical way, with mutual recognition of ministries and so on. Many of the hopes and aspirations of my generation have been dashed by the hard experience of the last quarter of a century. The Churches in Wales seem as far from uniting as ever, and for many the urgent and pressing issue is simply survival in the face of apathy, economic hardship and an ever-ageing membership.

I look at the Churches in Wales as someone nurtured in the Anglican tradition, but whose aspirations have always taken him in the direction of promoting the unity of all Christians in Wales in the cause of evangelism. I am also by conviction a Welsh nationalist, and so the context of Wales is of vital importance to me. Hopefully, my nationalism, like that of others in *Plaid Cymru*, is tempered by a strong internationalism and an enthusiastic pro-European outlook. By now bitter experience has led me to conclude that for most Christians in Wales the urgent, immediate and, for many, the only imperative is nothing more or less than survival. Gone are the dreams of one united Church of Wales as an integral part of catholic Christianity. This is a matter of great sadness to me. At the same time in the course of my work I come across many signs of hope for the future, though these are often to be discerned in groups working outside the framework (some would say straitjacket) of the institutional Churches.

I want to consider some of these signs of hope towards the end of this essay, but my first task is to analyse the wide variety of factors that have brought Christianity in Wales in its institutional form to the point where some observers quite properly ask if there will be a Church worthy of the name in Wales by the end of the twenty-first century.

Change and Decay—the Causes

As one might expect, many of the reasons for decline are internal to the life and activity (or lack of it) of the Churches themselves. But no Church exists in a vacuum. No Church can pretend that it is unaffected by the nature of the society in which it finds itself.

Church members, and they in the final analysis *are* the Church, live not only in the Church but in society. At certain points in the history of the Church various Churches or groups of Christians have sought to shut themselves off from society, usually on the basis of a theological conviction that the world is *inherently* sinful and evil. This is, of course, a denial of two of the great tenets of the Christian faith, the doctrine of Creation (that the world and everything in it is God's creation) and the doctrine of Incarnation (that God assumed human flesh and thereby made flesh and with it the whole material order a potential vehicle for the divine presence in the world). Nor have certain Christians in Wales been immune from this tendency to deny the world and human society—the Puritans and the Calvinistic Methodists would be prime examples.

By contrast, Christians in other parts of our world today have shown how powerful Christian witness in action can be in helping to transform society—the Churches in South Africa over the past quarter of a century or Christians in Eastern Europe over the past decade are outstanding examples.

No Church then can pretend that it exists in isolation from the society of which it is part. It can help shape that society, and the Church in turn is itself to some extent shaped by society. If society changes in any significant way, this almost inevitably has a knock-on effect on the Church. Similarly, if something dramatic happens to transform the Church—for example, a revival of the kind we in Wales have witnessed at intervals over the past two hundred and fifty years or an epoch-making event such as the Second Vatican Council, this in turn has an impact on society generally.

Over the course of the twentieth century changes in society in Wales have significantly affected the life of the Churches. It is perhaps a sad commentary on the fundamental theological and psychological weakness of the Churches in Wales that they have been so affected by changes in the society around them, but have themselves made little or no impact on the changing shape of Welsh society as it approaches the twenty-first century.

Nor is it economic, political and social change alone that influences the life of the Churches. Changes in cultural and intellectual fashion also make their mark. This has been true over the twenty centuries of the Church's existence as even a cursory examination of Church history will illustrate. Over the centuries Christians have adapted their message to the language, thought forms, even the ideologies of different societies in a sincere attempt to communicate what they see as the truths of salvation. Indeed, failure to communicate in this way invariably condemns the Church to a life at the margins of society. Yet this is a tightrope for the Churches to negotiate. Certainly they must seek to communicate in language and concepts that people understand, but there is always a danger that in adapting their basic message to new modes of expression the Churches will betray what they stand for and become so assimilated into the prevailing culture as to be indistinguishable from it. That way spells death for the Church, and as we shall see there is more than a suspicion that Christian preachers in Wales over the past century and a half have so identified themselves with Western culture, on the one hand, or the Welsh language and its culture, on the other, as to undermine the essential distinctiveness and basic catholicity of the Christian movement.

In what follows we shall examine first a range of social, economic and political changes in society in Wales that have seriously affected the life of the Churches. Then we shall explore various movements in intellectual and cultural fashion and the impact such fashions have had on the Church's witness. Finally, we shall look at the Churches themselves and ask to what extent their own internal life, organization and activity have brought them to the sorry pass in which they find themselves today. Throughout we shall need to be sensitive to the significant differences between one Church tradition and another. What may be true of the Nonconformist (Free) Churches may not be true of the Roman Catholic Church in Wales and vice versa.

Mass Communication, Mobility and the Destabilization of Society

Two of the most significant agents of social change in Wales, as in the rest of the developed world, in the second half of the

10

twentieth century are highly sophisticated transport systems, particularly designed for the private motor-car, and the explosive development of mass-media of communication (television, radio, telephone, fax and, more recently, computer-based electronic communication networks). As a consequence, our world has become very much smaller. We can travel physically around the world in less than twenty-four hours, and in our minds in seconds, particularly when stimulated by live TV pictures from the other side of the globe. We in Wales cannot but be aware that we are now part of an international community, that the world is at our feet, that as citizens of that world we can travel anywhere within it for work or for pleasure.

Even Wales itself, in spite of its comparatively underdeveloped road system, has become much smaller. In contrast to our ancestors who a century ago relied for the most part on horse-drawn transport, we can contemplate a return journey to any part of Wales as a comfortable day's excursion. This ease of mobility means that people nowadays are prepared to travel substantial distances to work, distances usually measured in time (say an hour) rather than in miles or kilometres (say fifty miles or eighty kilometres). And insofar as we have fast roads, such as the M4, they connect Wales to England with unprecedented ease. The Welsh can as rapidly leave Wales for work in England as the English can enter Wales in search of an alternative lifestyle, with its perceived enhancement of their quality of life. Within Wales work now tends to be concentrated in particular locations away from residential areas, in industrial estates, office blocks, out-of-town shopping complexes and so on. As a consequence, many, if not most, villages in Wales and most valley communities are now little more than dormitories or holiday retreats.

Of course, ours is not the first generation that has had to move to find work. In my own family some members of my grand-parents' generation left west Wales to settle in the Rhondda at the turn of the century. In the middle part of this century three of my father's family of eight ended up working in England and two others in parts of Wales away from their native village. What is different now is the dramatic increase in mobility, which is such that many Welsh communities are inhabited by a majority of

11

immigrants, either from other parts of Wales or more often from England. Those of us who choose to move leave behind us our roots, our extended families and our sense of belonging, thenceforth to wander as professional élite mercenaries in a rootless society.

Education, which over the years has been so highly prized by the Welsh as the means to a better life, has in the event deprived most communities in rural Wales of their ablest daughters and sons. This has in some cases dealt a fatal blow to any sense of community among those who remain. Families are scattered, and in their new environment people rarely maintain the traditions and habits of their former community life. This loss of a sense of community, together with the break-up of families and a new rootless existence, has had a profound destabilizing effect on society as a whole, and we in Wales, like our fellows in countries around the world, are as yet some way from resolving the consequential social problems.

At the same time the mass-media of communication have brought the world into our living-rooms, even our bedrooms. We can now see how the other half lives; in some ways this is a salutary experience since our generation knows more about the suffering, poverty and deprivation that afflict millions of our fellow human beings than did our parents or grandparents. We now have no excuse for indifference to the injustices and inequalities of our global community. But this is not, of course, the whole story. Frequently television presents a romantic, glamorous picture of life, which raises expectations and exacerbates frustration, tension and discontent among the have-nots. Television advertisements aimed at children are a particularly pernicious influence in society since they cruelly heighten awareness of their own social deprivation among the innocent victims of economic injustice.

As for religion, the media have made us in Wales more aware than ever before that there are many different religions, many different ways to God, in the world around us. We are aware of the great variety of ideologies and philosophies of life espoused by our fellow human beings. All this tends to undermine the old certainties, to foster doubt and to encourage experiment. Not

12

surprisingly, therefore, even in Wales a not insignificant number of people are attracted to what are generally seen as exotic cults. Furthermore, immigration into Wales has brought other faiths and other philosophies into our midst in a concrete, personal form. We are now familiar with real-life Muslims or Hindus or Buddhists, who at one time seemed so different from the rest of us, and no longer see the Jews as a misguided religious group too stubborn to convert to Christianity. Where earlier generations were simply curious about the variety of denominational traditions within Christianity, our children do not take any religious allegiance for granted and are as likely to ask, 'Do you have any religious belief?' as the traditional Welsh question, 'What denomination do you belong to?'

All these developments have transformed out of all recognition not only the stereotypical caricature, but also the reality of life in rural villages and valley communities throughout Wales. I was brought up in a rural village in the 1940s. In that community my sister and I were seen as exceptional in that our roots lay elsewhere. The majority of our fellow pupils in the village school came from families who for generations had been born, lived and died in that same local community. This, it seems to me, was true of most rural communities in Wales up until the middle part of this century. It gave stability and a sense of belonging to those who lived in those communities. To find your roots, you needed only to visit the graveyard, where you could trace the history of your family over many generations on the tombstones. You could call on your extended family in time of need, and were even drawn willy-nilly into family feuds extending over decades! The same was true of valley communities and even of conurbations like Swansea, where I worked in the mid-1960s and which was still at that time more a collection of villages than a modern cosmopolitan urban centre. Professor Chris Harris's sociological studies of the region simply confirmed for me the subjective impression gained on visiting homes around Swansea that nine out of ten of its inhabitants had been born there and that the vast majority of them intended to die there.

Now not all of this was good and we must beware of the Welsh disease of romanticizing the past in a glow of *hiraeth*. These

13

communities may have been stable; their inhabitants may have had roots to give them a sense of belonging, but often they were introverted, static, economically undeveloped, intolerant and incestuous (in my experience of rural life, they were sometimes quite literally incestuous). My main point is not that these communities were wholly good and that our society today is wholly bad, but that these communities gave Welsh society a basic stability and gave Welsh people a sense of belonging, of having roots.

Part of this stability was provided by the Church, whatever the denomination, since as far as the Free Churches are concerned the denomination varied from place to place. Sunday worship, baptisms, marriages and funerals, celebrations of seedtime and harvest, were all part of an ordered and orderly way of life. Now with many of the indigenous, upwardly mobile population moving out and with immigrant newcomers taking their place, this way of life is rapidly disintegrating and with it the central place of the Church in people's lives. Sunday is now a day for going on trips, visiting people and places, shopping, watching or playing sport and the like, a time for relaxation, for the family even, but not for worship. Just as the supermarket caters for the needs of our mobile population more successfully than the local corner or village shop, so a new supermarket of religions and ideologies now offers a more exciting variety of novel experiences, which the undeveloped and rundown local corner shop of a church cannot match.

Of the mainline denominations in Wales the Free Churches are the major losers in all this change. This is in the main because they have been both by theological conviction and in practical expression *local* churches. When people move out, they tend to forfeit their membership not only of their local Church, but of the Church itself. The Anglican Church in Wales with its developed network of parishes and the Roman Catholic Church with its strong emphasis on membership of a worldwide community have withstood and even benefited from these changes. Indeed, it may not be without significance that the Roman Catholic Church is one of the few Christian traditions that is numerically stronger in Wales today than it was a century ago.

Anglicization and Cultural Assimilation

Increased mobility and the pervading influence of the mass-media have had other more radical consequences for society in Wales. As each year passes, and notwithstanding an increased national awareness and self-confidence in some circles, Wales becomes less distinctive; gradually we are becoming more like the region of England that some perceive us to be and more closely assimilated to a monochrome 'Western' way of thinking and a characterless North Atlantic pattern of life.

I remember being totally astonished when I first moved to Lampeter a quarter of a century ago to find adult monoglot Welsh-speakers in the area. Though my immediate family on both sides had to a man and, more volubly, to a woman been thoroughly Welsh-speaking, all of them spoke English as well. I was even more amazed to find elderly people in villages around Lampeter who had never seen the sea; some of them, living no more than five miles away, had never even been to Lampeter. This now seems totally incredible. It reflects a different world, the world of the nineteenth more than of the twentieth century. It was a world where people quite naturally lived all their lives through the medium of the Welsh language, which in the final analysis is the most distinctive feature of Wales.

The steady decline in the number of Welsh-speakers over the course of the twentieth century may be traced statistically through census returns, as may the effects of the heroic efforts of educationalists and others in more recent years to arrest the decline with an encouraging degree of success. Yet when all is said and done it has to be recognized that Welsh is now the language of a relatively small minority (one in five) of the inhabitants of Wales, where at the turn of the century it was spoken by a majority. A further and more significant change over the past thirty or so years has been the marked redistribution of Welsh-speakers away from the rural areas into the urban centres, especially Cardiff. No more can we realistically speak of *y Fro Gymraeg*, a Welsh-speaking heartland. There are few natural Welsh-speaking communities left in rural Wales, as I can testify from the personal experience of living and working in rural

15

Dyfed for over a quarter of a century. Immigration and the influence of the mass-media have changed the face of rural Wales linguistically and culturally as well as socially and economically. By contrast, the community of Welsh-speakers in Cardiff is now probably stronger than it has ever been, but it exists as a community within a community, almost as a ghetto, and tends either to adopt an introverted and defensive ghetto-mentality or more commonly to become assimilated in all respects other than language into the lifestyle and attitudes of the wider community of which it is part.

Such cultural and social assimilation is not, however, confined to Cardiff. All over Wales people tend now to think and behave more like the English than ever before. This is hardly surprising when we think of the constant stream of English 'propaganda' that comes into our homes day after day and night after night. Notwithstanding the outstanding service of BBC Radio Cymru and the well-meaning efforts of S4C, such provision can hardly compare either in quantity or in quality with numerous round-the-clock radio and TV channels that are English-based or with the ready daily availability of broadsheets and tabloids published in London. The effects of all this can be discerned in many ways. In terms of politics, for example, large parts of Wales now conform to 'national' voting patterns as never before, even if the Celtic fringe still stubbornly asserts its independence. Or if we think of leisure activities or even eating habits we in Wales are as likely, indeed more likely, to raid the local video shop or to frequent the local bistro as we are to attend an Eisteddfod or a *Noson Lawen*.

But the extent of our cultural emasculation is much deeper than this. Even when we speak Welsh, we tend to reflect the same attitudes and to think the same thoughts as others all over the Western, Anglo-American world. We are, of course, by no means unique in this respect. Even as fiercely culturally independent a people as the French are worried about the insidious influence of that North Atlantic culture, of which (American) English is the linguistic medium.

One of the characteristics of a media-generated culture and the society it creates is its superficiality. 'Here today and gone

16

tomorrow' is its watchword. No one is interested in yesterday's news, nor is anyone interested in anything that is less than sensational. Scandal is the order of the day. We live in an age of soundbites, which is informed more by ephemeral appeal than by history and tradition. Wales is as much a part of and indeed victim of this culture as anywhere else in the Western world.

Yet the changes have hit Wales harder than most, because we are a small country with a culture that was for centuries inextricably bound up with a distinctive, but minority language unknown to all intents and purposes outside the territory of the community that spoke it. Moreover, this language owed its continuing existence to the all-pervading influence of the Christian Church. It is universally acknowledged that the critical turning-point in the history of the Welsh language was the translation of the Bible into Welsh in the second half of the sixteenth century. Thereafter the Welsh Bible became the standard for literary Welsh and the textbook for generations of Welsh people, for whom the Protestant faith was their whole way of life.

As a consequence, some Christian denominations in Wales have been and continue to be exclusively Welsh-speaking: for example, Undeb yr Annibynwyr Cymraeg (the Union of Welsh Independents) or the Welsh Baptist Union. The Calvinistic Methodist or Presbyterian Church of Wales is also very largely a Welsh-speaking Church. The enormous growth of this peculiarly Welsh Nonconformity in the nineteenth century resulted in literally thousands of Chapels being built all over Wales. Correspondingly, the decline of Welsh Nonconformity has resulted in the sale or pitiful dilapidation of hundreds, if not thousands, of these Chapels over the past thirty or so years. The fortunes of the language have been mirrored in the fortunes of those denominations who had so identified with the language as to cease to be truly catholic. To this extent, the Anglican Church in Wales, with its bilingual tradition, though one it has frequently betrayed, and the Roman Catholic Church in Wales have been better able to adapt to the linguistic and cultural change of the second half of the twentieth century, as have the burgeoning

Pentecostal and evangelical Churches that are modelled on a North American pattern.

Individualism and Materialism

Another of the dominant features of modern Western society which we in Wales reflect is its materialism. In such a society everything is measured in terms of its material value. Success is marked by the wealth of material trappings it brings—a large house, complete with swimming pool and jacuzzi, a fast car with a mobile phone, holidays in exotic faraway locations and the like. This may be an exaggerated caricature, and it is certainly beyond the reach of most people in Wales, but this sort of material success is presented as the pinnacle of achievement or, as often as not, good fortune: for example, a win on the National Lottery, the new institution that epitomizes this attitude to life.

Much of the credit for this quite dramatic rise in people's expectations and attitudes as to what constitutes human happiness and self-fulfilment must be attributed to the Thatcher government of the 1980s. Whether we approve of these developments or not, we have to acknowledge that by a series of cleverly designed measures aimed at the basest human instinct, self-interest, Margaret Thatcher and her government succeeded in bringing about a revolution in social attitudes and in creating a property and share-owning populace with a strong vested interest in preserving the kind of capitalist system represented by Thatcherite conservatism. Even her bitterest enemies have to admire the thoroughness of this achievement. We in Wales, to judge from our voting habits, may not have liked or supported Thatcherism, but not one of us is unaffected by it.

One of Margaret Thatcher's more memorable pronouncements was this: 'There is no such thing as society'. In other words, human interaction is a matter of everyone for themselves; this is no more than a sophisticated version of the law of the jungle. This pronouncement does, however, remind us that Thatcherite conservatism is founded on a powerful ideology, the ideology of individualism.

As R. H. Tawney showed clearly in his seminal work *Religion and the Rise of Capitalism*, Western capitalism, of which Thatcherite conservatism is a particularly powerful manifestation, has its roots in the kind of Protestant Christianity, with its strong work-ethic, that developed on the continent of Europe, notably among Dutch Calvinists, as a consequence of the Reformation. This form of Christianity laid great emphasis on the individual, on the need for personal commitment on the part of the individual and on individual responsibility over against the excessive collectivism that characterized Western Catholicism. This then produced an expectation that God would reward the individual in proportion to that individual's faith, industry and effort. Such a 'theology of success' is now advanced in a more sophisticated form in the modern world among fundamentalist Protestant groups in the USA and through their influence in the rapidly expanding Calvinistic Protestant Churches in South Korea. Success is seen as evidence of God's reward for those Christians who industriously pursue the Protestant work-ethic, and failure correspondingly is interpreted as God's punishment of sin or idleness. The poor are therefore poor by reason of their own failure (sin).

In keeping with this theology, which is then incorporated into the ideology of capitalism, the individual must take full responsibility for his (or her) actions. Each of us is master of his fate. We may have to accept responsibility for our immediate family and dependents, but since there is no such thing as society, the individual has no real social responsibility, nor is there such a thing as social, i.e. collective, sin. That this pernicious ideology is based on Calvinism is a sad reflection on the perversion of Christian theology that emanated from some of the Protestant Reformers, who in this respect succeeded in throwing out the baby with the bathwater in a big way.

Over the past decade this ideology has dominated society in Wales, as of course has Calvinism at other times in our history, so the phenomenon is not entirely new. Materialistic aspirations fuelled and justified by the ideology of individualism are as evident in Wales as they are in other parts of the Western so-called developed world. What is ironical from the point of view

19

of Protestant Churches in the Calvinist tradition is that their particular brand of Protestant theology sowed the seeds of the destruction of the very institutions (the Churches) that exist to direct human attention away from the pursuit of material success to an awareness of 'spiritual' values and the 'divine' dimension of human existence and of the whole created order. In such a climate to preach 'the option for the poor' is likely to fall on deaf ears.

In such circumstances the Churches have two options: either they compromise and espouse the kind of 'theology of success' adopted by some Protestant Churches in the USA and South Korea, which are materially very wealthy, or they can continue to proclaim the essential justice of the God of the Bible, who is the defender of 'the fatherless and widow', and the all-embracing and selfless love of God incarnate in 'the man for others'. If the Churches adopt the latter course, as to their credit they have done on many continents, notably Latin America, they face the prospect of being marginalized along with the poor. This is the dilemma that confronts the Churches in Wales in our contemporary materialistic and individualistic environment. In terms of their theological traditions it will be easier for Churches in the 'catholic' tradition to respond positively than for those whose theology is deeply imbued with Calvinism.

Prevailing Intellectual and Cultural Influences on Society

Children and young people in Wales today enjoy the advantages of an educational system which is universally available to those between the ages of five and sixteen and for many well beyond that, and for those in school this education is free. Though the links between primary and secondary education, on the one hand, and higher education, on the other, are not always clear, they are mutually inter-dependent. The one feeds off the other in that the schools produce the students for higher education, and higher education, in its turn, produces the teachers for the schools. There are, of course, those who go through this educational system in their formative years without being discernibly

20

affected by it, but the vast majority are deeply and fundamentally influenced by what they receive and learn as part of their formal education, and this in turn affects the way society thinks.

Some Churches have a long record of being sensitive to the fundamental importance of education for shaping society. This is particularly true of the Roman Catholic Church and for most of the past two hundred or more years of the Anglican Church as well, though recently Anglicans have ceded much of this responsibility to the state. Church schools are, however, in a minority; for the majority the education they receive is secular and under the control of the state (in Wales in the form of the Welsh Office), but even in Church schools the approach to the study of almost every subject in the curriculum is thoroughly secular, since the teachers have been trained and educated in a higher education system which is almost exclusively informed by rationalist and secularist principles.

In seeking to analyze how society in Wales thinks we therefore need to examine the basic principles of the philosophy that undergirds our present educational system, since consciously or unconsciously we in Wales are all heavily influenced by these philosophical ideas and their underlying assumptions. To a greater or lesser extent they affect our whole attitude to what it means to be human. We are not, of course, unique in this respect, since the same is true of most other countries around the world. Control of education, like control of the mass media, is basic to control of the way society develops. On occasions we can see very clearly the impact of this manipulation of education to effect changes in society and people's attitudes—for example, in the crude efforts of socialist regimes in Eastern Europe earlier in this century to impose a particular ideology (Marxism) on society. But in criticizing the single-minded ruthlessness of the Marxist in this respect, we should remember that no educational system is value-free. This again is something Thatcherite conservatives, such as Dr Redwood, understand only too well. All of us are in some measure and often to a considerable degree creatures of our education. Why else do some parents pay such huge sums of money to secure educational advantage for their children? In that sense the recent emphasis on education as a life-

21

long experience is a welcome and salutary development, since education is then more likely to become the self-correcting process it should be.

So what are the underlying principles on which our educational system here in Wales is based and how does this impact on the ability of the Churches to persuade the people of Wales to believe in what they proclaim? To understand these principles more clearly we need to examine the rationalism and secularism of which modern education is a by-product, as well as the liberalism and pluralism which have at different times formed the cultural context in which the educational system operates.

Rationalism and Secularism

The roots of rationalism as such may be traced to continental philosophers of the sixteenth and seventeenth centuries, such as René Descartes. Also relevant in the long term are the British empiricists, such as David Hume, of roughly the same period, since their work also helped lay the foundations for the rejection of otherworldly explanations that later characterized the Age of Reason. Mathematical reasoning was the paradigm for Descartes' system of knowledge; his philosophical method, the method of doubt, was characterized by starting from scratch without any prior assumptions, such as the existence of God. Hume, on the other hand, laid great emphasis on experience; consequently what is contrary to normal human experience of the natural world is unacceptable to the human mind—miracles would be a prime example.

As refined in what is called the Age of Reason rationalism asserts that all claims, including theological claims, must be submitted to the test of human reason and if found wanting they must be rejected. Similarly, solutions to the questions and problems posed by human existence can only be reached by the application of human reason. Since most religions, and particularly Christianity, base their central claims on revealed truth, which humans must either accept or reject, there is a fundamental tension between rationalism and religion, between reason and faith.

Rationalist influence led to the development of the even more sceptical secularism in the nineteenth century, though moves in this direction can be traced as far back as the Renaissance. The secularist sets out to interpret everything on principles derived solely from this world and as a consequence deliberately ignores the God-hypothesis or belief in another order of existence (eternal life, for example). This can then develop into out-and-out atheism, though not necessarily so. Many of those who campaigned for social reform or who advocated revolution in the last century were secularists, even if they are not normally described as such. The most notable example would be Karl Marx with his materialist (i.e. secularist) philosophy, which was aggressively atheistic, since Marx saw religion as a massive hindrance to the establishment of a more just social and economic order.

On the face of it our educational system is hardly atheistic. Indeed, religious education is compulsory, but on closer examination it becomes clear that this gives a totally misleading impression. The essential point is that God and the supernatural are consciously and deliberately excluded from all modern academic disciplines following their espousal of what is called the 'scientific' method. Popularly this is thought only to affect science. Consequently, it occasions no surprise that God finds no place in the theories of physics (how the universe began, for example) or biology (how did life begin, for example). The truth is, however, that there is no room for God in the study of history or economics either, nor is there any reference to the notion of God's law in the academic study of law or the training of lawyers. Indeed, even theology has adopted a scientific approach—for example, to the study of the Bible, which academically is examined according to the same principles as any other work of literature or any other historical document.

The inevitable consequence of all this is that we are conditioned by our education, which for many of us embraces the twenty or so most formative years of our lives, to look at life and human existence without resort to explanations outside the experience of our material order since such explanations are not susceptible to the tests of reason. In such circumstances the

Churches seem doomed to fight a losing battle against the massed forces of secularism, and the real question is perhaps how they have survived at all.

Theologians and Church leaders have not, however, stood on one side as inactive spectators of all this; many have attempted to accommodate the faith to the intellectual context of our modern, secular society. As an academic theologian I was trained in a tradition that reflected this 'liberal' response, and Lampeter can, proudly or otherwise, claim to have been a centre of what we may call, for want of a better word, 'liberalism' within the Anglican tradition, just as other centres in Wales and elsewhere have come to represent liberal Protestantism or liberal Catholicism. So does this approach succeed in arresting what otherwise seems to be a headlong descent into oblivion for the Churches in Wales?

Liberalism

Liberalism is not, of course, a new phenomenon. For well over a century, Christian theologians, though at first only a small and persecuted minority, theologians like Rowland Williams, one of my predecessors at Lampeter, in the mid-nineteenth century, have been wrestling with the need to reconcile or at least to resolve the conflict between the received (and revealed) truths of the faith, as articulated in the Bible and the Creeds, for example, and the results of human intellectual endeavour.

In essence a liberal approach means a readiness to welcome new ideas and to promote change through reform rather than revolution. Those of a liberal disposition favour freedom and open-mindedness and despise what they see as bigotry and prejudice. Liberal theologians therefore tend to be anti-dogmatic and this naturally brings them into conflict with Church authorities, particularly in the case of a highly centralized Church like the Roman Catholic Church, as can be seen clearly in the attitude of the Vatican to a theologian like the German Professor Hans Kung. In practice, most Churches have a liberal wing, which finds itself in tension, if not open conflict, with the conservative forces (usually the majority) within that Church, who accuse the liberals of compromising the faith to the point where it becomes indistinguishable from humanism or whatever other-ism seems fashionable at the time.

Liberals within the Churches have concentrated in the main on doctrinal beliefs and ethical principles. Belief in a six-day creation or in the fall as an historical event is reinterpreted in terms of accepting general truths about God as creator and humanity as sinful. Literal belief in the virginal conception of Jesus or in his physical resurrection is demythologised and re-presented as an affirmation of his divine origin or his final triumph in some spiritual sense over evil and death. Similarly, in terms of ethical teaching the liberal tendency is to avoid absolute pronouncements and to judge each particular case on its merits and in the light of the prevailing circumstances. Abortion, for example, is not necessarily to be seen as evil in all circumstances, and according to many liberals may in certain circumstances be morally justified.

Such reinterpretation of the faith has, as noted above, been going on for some time. It is now the dominant element in most British University departments of theology and indeed in many theological colleges. It has therefore had a not insignificant influence on the pulpit. This has predictably provoked a sharp reaction from those who see it as undermining the true faith. Whether it undermines or helps to sustain the true faith is a matter of debate, but what must now be admitted (and I speak as an erstwhile 'liberal' turned radical theologian) is that a liberal approach has been no more successful in its appeal than the old unreconstructed conservative tradition. Indeed, there is evidence that the proclamation of the full-blown gospel now has a wider appeal than the watered-down version of liberalism. People's reluctance to accept the Christian gospel is not really a matter of intellectual difficulties; the real stumbling-block is the degree of commitment required to a particular way of life and the threat this poses to self-interest and self-gratification. Growth is now evident in conservative, evangelical Churches, particularly in urban areas in Wales. The growing popularity of the Roman

Catholic Church in Wales may also be not unrelated to its predilection for dogma and unambiguous teaching.

Having said all that, it remains true, of course, that the bulk of the population of Wales have deserted the faith of their forebears to the extent that they are no longer afraid of hell or similar sanctions beyond the grave, and this in turn may be reflected in the permissive (some would say tolerant) nature of much of Welsh society. In that sense the liberals have won the argument, even if they have not succeeded in keeping hold on the faithful. What I suspect we shall see, however, as we enter the new millennium, is a smaller number of increasingly conservative Churches serving a dwindling minority of highly committed faithful.

Pluralism

The tolerance of a variety of different beliefs that characterizes liberalism has encouraged the growth in recent times of religious pluralism within the context of a multicultural society. Such a pluralist approach to the study and practice of religion has influenced the teaching of religious education in schools, and this of course is the trend Dr Redwood and others in his party wish to reverse. His Christmas 1994 promulgation is simply one of a series of government statements expressing disquiet about what they see as the too rapid acceptance of religious pluralism.

In its pure form religious pluralism means that all religions are regarded as equally valid ways to God. No attempt is made to adjudicate between the various truth claims of the different faiths, since each faith is considered to be 'true' for those who believe in it. That religion has a long and unenviable record of generating conflict, even war, is beyond dispute. This is because people generally hold very deep convictions in relation to their religious faith, convictions they are willing to defend to the death, if necessary, or in other extreme cases to impose on others by brute force. Christians in particular have a shameful record in this respect, as may be seen in the history of continents like India, Africa and especially Latin America.

What the advocates of religious pluralism therefore hope to achieve is better understanding and consequently greater tolerance between the adherents of different faiths both on a world scale and locally here at home. Until recently the co-existence of different religions hardly seemed an issue in Wales, but it is now evident that Wales too is very much part of the one multi-faith, multi-cultured modern world.

The political and social advantages of securing greater tolerance between the adherents of different faiths are self-evident, but for the committed Christian, like the committed Muslim or the committed Hindu, the cost of pluralism sometimes seems too high a price to pay since it carries with it the implication that since all faiths are of equal validity no one faith has an exclusive claim to truth; there is also a tacit understanding that neither Churches nor other faith communities will proselytise, and for Christians this is a denial of one of the imperatives of the gospel.

In general, broad Churches like the Anglican Church or Churches in the liberal Protestant tradition have found it easier to accommodate religious pluralism than have hardliners in the Roman Catholic Church (notwithstanding the openness of Vatican II towards adherents of other faiths) or Churches in the conservative evangelical tradition, for whom all talk of pluralism is anathema.

The Life of the Churches Themselves

In turning finally to the Churches themselves we must acknowledge that, however significant the impact on the Churches of the social and intellectual trends we have discussed, the Churches themselves bear some responsibility for the persistent decline in popular appeal they have experienced over the course of the twentieth century. Our next task, therefore, is to analyze internal features of the life of the Churches that have been contributory factors in this decline.

Institutionalization and Professionalization

A phenomenon well-known to psychologists is the inability of some who have been confined for long periods in institutions, whether hospitals, residential schools, prisons or even religious communities, after a time to face life in the outside world. Their pattern of institutional life is so secure and well-ordered that they are afraid of the responsibility of looking after themselves in an alien and apparently unfriendly environment; they are even afraid of the prospect of having to think for themselves. This condition very closely describes the state of many of our institutional Churches. They have ceased to look out; they exist for themselves; their primary concern is with internal matters—for example, the ordination of women to the priesthood, discussions over Church unity, internal organizational issues and the like. Consequently, these Churches have turned in on themselves. They are comfortable places for committed members, but unwelcoming to outsiders and there is no real attempt to encourage others to join them. Ironically in this the so-called 'decade of evangelism' the Churches have given up on evangelism. Evangelism is left to the para-Church organizations of evangelists like Dr Billy Graham.

All this spells death for the Protestant Churches. The Reformation in the sixteenth century was very largely a revolt against the shortcomings of the (Roman Catholic) Church as an institution. An outbreak of enthusiasm, widely interpreted as a movement of the spirit, followed the break with Rome. This was even more true of the Methodist revival in Wales in the eighteenth century led by enthusiasts like Howell Harris, Daniel Rowland and William Williams (Pantycelyn), as it was true of later revivals—for example, the revival of 1904. Such enthusiasm was contagious; it attracted hundreds, if not thousands, of followers. It was an enthusiasm that reflected an emotional rather than an intellectual response, and the resultant excitement and commitment to God it generated contrasted with the staid, stereotyped forms of worship that characterized the traditional Churches the Reformers and the Revivalists left behind—the Church of Rome and the Church of England.

28

It is therefore very sad that today it is the worship of the Reformed Churches that has become stereotyped, staid and lifeless in comparison with the revised forms of worship of the traditional Churches from whom they broke away. One cannot but conclude that the life has gone out of the mainline Free Churches in Wales, and their lifelessness is made worse because they have no rich, liturgical tradition on which to fall back, unlike the Roman Catholic and Anglican Churches, which have both been revived by liturgical reform in the second part of the twentieth century. Lively, enthusiastic worship is indeed found within the Protestant tradition, but in the newer evangelical, charismatic and Pentecostal Churches that have imitated North American patterns. Institutionalization has killed the spirit of enthusiasm that was the lifeblood of Welsh Nonconformity. Though we can understand what motivated the Reformers to break with Rome or the Revivalists to leave the Church of England, from the perspective of the late twentieth century we are forced to conclude that the Protestant Reformation and the Methodist Revival in the final analysis weakened both Christian witness in Wales and Welsh awareness of independent nationality. The contrast with the Irish Republic is telling in this respect. Ireland is still both strongly Christian and fiercely proud of its independent nationality, and the Irish experience indicates what might have been if the history of Wales had taken a different turn in the sixteenth century.

Another aspect of the institutionalization of the Churches is the professionalization of a clerical (ordained) élite. This has always been a traditional feature of the order of the Roman Catholic and Anglican Churches, and as interpreted historically it has meant the exclusion of women from ministry, to the serious detriment of both Church and society. It also tends to result in the exclusion of the laity; this seems true even in the Free Churches. We have seen, for example, a 'clerical' monopoly on biblical interpretation, something that academic theology has, perhaps unwittingly, encouraged. Over the past hundred years the letters BA, BD have been widely regarded as essential qualifications for interpreting the word of God. It is a paradox that Churches in the Reformed, Protestant tradition, the tradition originally responsible for opening the Bible to the whole people of God and encouraging them to read and interpret the Scriptures for themselves, have conspired in their institutional form to take responsibility for interpreting the Bible away from the people by concentrating it in the hands of a professional élite of trained and authorized preachers. That this system is now breaking down for financial reasons may be a sign of God's displeasure.

Be that as it may, the Roman Catholic Church has as a consequence of the liturgical revolution brought about by the Second Vatican Council (1962-1965) not only caught up with, but in some respects surpassed the achievements of the Reformers; the consequences of this are now becoming evident all over the Catholic world and are, sometimes to the disquiet of the Vatican itself, both unpredictable and uncontrollable. The Roman Catholic Church and the Church in Wales, with their developed threefold ministry of bishops, priests and deacons, also seem better able to sustain and justify a professional core of ordained clergy since with their more advanced theology of the Church, they give it a proper historical and social context in the life of both Church and society. What these Churches seem unable to resolve, however, is how to utilize the talents of women and the laity in the ministry of the whole Church as it seeks to serve contemporary society in Wales.

Rejection of the Legacy of Puritanism

The Sunday Trading Act 1994 removed the last vestiges of the traditional Welsh 'Sabbath', that symbol of the Puritan influence on Welsh society that was at the same time a satirist's dream and a tourist's nightmare. Most of us in Wales over the age of forty can think of a time not too long ago when Sunday (or as it was wrongly termed the Sabbath) was literally a day of rest in the sense of inactivity. No shopping! No drinking in public houses! No sport! No dancing! No cinema! No hanging washing on the line! No nothing! This was the high point of the negative influence on Wales of the Puritanism which represented the essence of Welsh Nonconformity. The zealots, of course, believed in the value of all this, but most Welsh people were schizophrenic in their attitude to it. While giving public approval, or at least tacit assent, in private they ignored it and even despised it. The Welsh Sunday and along with it Chapel society has been cruelly caricatured, even lampooned, not least by the Welsh themselves, many of whom have experienced a perverse thrill at the mild rebellion of playing cricket or drinking a pint of beer on a Sunday. This later turned to out-and-out rejection of this world-denying form of Christianity.

Successive plebiscites on the Sunday opening of public houses and recent legislation on Sunday trading have now consigned all this to the dustbin of history. The Welsh now drink alcohol openly on Sundays as on other days, and with disturbing frequency to excess. The problem of alcohol abuse is widespread, but is now countered with teaching about the potential damage to physical health and to domestic life rather than with warnings about hell fire as punishment for the sin of drunkenness.

As a matter of fact, neither the Roman Catholic Church nor the Church in Wales set any great store by the traditional Welsh Sunday. The problem for the Free Churches, however, has been that they have expended considerable energy in one last-ditch defence campaign after another, first against the Sunday opening of public houses, then against Sunday sport and other entertainment and finally against Sunday trading. In fighting these battles they were out of step with public opinion, with the result that in rejecting the Welsh Sunday and all it represented, the Welsh public at the same time rejected the Puritanical form of Christianity that supported it.

We now have the total paradox of hearing Welsh hymns of the temperance movement sung with gusto in village taverns around Welsh Wales, where the Chapel Choirs of total abstainers have long since been silenced. A whole way of life is passing, and in most respects has already passed, leaving a spiritual vacuum. We shall have to see how the Roman Catholic and the Anglican Churches respond to this challenge, since with the exception of the burgeoning evangelical movement, which cuts across denominational allegiances, the mainstream Free Churches have little or nothing left to offer.

Collective Loss of Confidence

A common response of teenagers and young people generally when asked about their experience of what goes on in Church or Chapel is to say that it is 'boring'. If we are honest, many of us who are somewhat older would echo these sentiments. One of the chief reasons for this is that those who lead worship and particularly those who preach seem simply to be going through a series of traditional and time-honoured motions. The preaching is often tired, cliché-ridden and lacking in both inspiration and conviction. If the *hoelion wyth*, the pulpit stars of the earlier part of the century, knew how to entertain their hearers, their late twentieth-century successors have long since lost the art.

This is sad since in my experience ministers and clergy are sincere, devout and good people who command general respect. Yet their public persona is often lacking in confidence and this is then reflected in their preaching. In my younger days I derived considerable enjoyment from playing a variety of sports and came to learn a great deal about human nature in the process. A key ingredient in those who perform at the highest level of sport is self-confidence, belief in their ability to do what they are doing and to do it better than others. Without confidence a batsman in cricket has a disastrous run of scores or a placekicker in rugby football finds that he misses more often than not, even though in both cases the individual has all the necessary talent and skill in abundance. The same is true of other walks of life. So for a preacher, as for a politician, lack of confidence is the kiss of death. Not only has he ceased to believe in himself; he has also to all outward appearances ceased to believe in the power of God to inspire him.

What then is the cause of this collective loss of nerve among the clergy, the leaders of the mainline Churches, a loss of nerve that contrasts sharply with the total conviction that characterizes the preaching of the newer evangelical Churches? Why are the ordained ministers of the traditional denominations so apparently tired and lifeless?

One obvious answer is that they are caught up in a vicious circle. Dwindling attendances sap their self-confidence, and this lack of confidence accelerates the decline in attendance. This is certainly a major factor, but it is by no means the only reason.

Perhaps the most powerful reason for the tired, exhausted face of the Churches, especially the Free Churches, is that so much of the time of full-time stipendiary ministers is taken up with the thankless task of keeping the show on the road financially, a role ministers are often ill-equipped to undertake and one which is hardly a fitting role for someone trained for preaching and pastoral work. With the exception of the Roman Catholic Church, which is fortunate in this respect, all the mainline Churches are bowed down under the burden of having too much 'plant' to maintain, a legacy of the expansive building programmes of Christians in the Victorian age. The cost of upkeep is now astronomical and imposes a well-nigh intolerable burden on the dwindling numbers of the faithful. To its credit the Presbyterian Church of Wales seems about to tackle this problem in a radical way by disposing of a substantial portion of its redundant plant, though one suspects it may turn out to be too little, too late.

The worry and anxiety associated with all this tends to fall chiefly on the clergy. Add to it the ever-increasing cost of maintaining a stipendiary ministry and the consequences are well-nigh fatal. The stress levels of clergy are increasing at an alarming rate. There is frequent talk of clergy 'burn-out'. Many leave the full-time employment of the Church and are often lost to the ministry; their families too suffer from the stress this antiquated system imposes. The burden of raising money has for many, if not a majority, become virtually intolerable, and this is reflected in a widespread loss of nerve, with its attendant feelings of hopelessness and helplessness.

A further reason is that as a consequence of the liberalism which has so strongly influenced academic theology, ministers are sometimes confused as to what exactly they believe. There is, in other words, a crisis of belief in some circles. At the same time ordinary people are looking for firm answers and clear guidance from the preacher, and this is sometimes where those trained in a liberal tradition find themselves at a loss. Living with religious doubt or even maintaining a reverent agnosticism is seldom comfortable, particularly when there is pressure to produce clear, sometimes simplistic, answers to complex theological problems. It may not be a coincidence that Churches which boast a conservative theology are more popular in their appeal, no doubt because their preaching carries conviction. Anglicans are perhaps better able to cope with theological doubt than the Free Churches because they lay greater emphasis on having a reasonable faith and also because within the context of the whole liturgy there is less emphasis on the sermon. Roman Catholics are also well equipped to cope with the pressures of living in a sceptical age since they tend to have fewer doubts about the essentials of their faith than liberal Protestants, and are therefore better able to give more definite answers to their followers.

In drawing to a close this analysis of the social, intellectual and internal ecclesiastical factors that have led to the twentieth-century decline in Church affiliation and attendance in Wales, we can now offer a kind of 'end of term' (or perhaps 'end of millennium') report on the various denominational traditions.

The Anglican Church in Wales has suffered less than the Free Churches, probably because it is a broad Church and, secondly, because its 'establishment' outlook enables it the more easily to accommodate itself to the prevailing social, political and cultural context. Developments like greater mobility and increasing Anglicization do no real harm to the Anglican Church with its perceived English orientation and its well-established parochial network. The Free Churches, however, seem to be in serious decline and our analysis suggests that the decline may be irreversible. Wesleyan Methodism, which was never a significant force in Wales, is all but extinct in large areas of Wales. This is rapidly becoming true of the tradition represented by the distinctively Welsh Baptist Union, though a number of English Baptist Churches are flourishing in some of the urban areas. The once strong Presbyterian (Calvinistic Methodist) Church (*yr Hen Gorff*) is also in serious difficulties, as are Churches in the Welsh Independent tradition. With no prospect of a revival these traditions will probably become significantly weaker, possibly to the point of extinction, in the coming century. Nor is there any real indication that the relatively new United Reformed Church is faring any better.

The Roman Catholic Church, on the other hand, is now in a strong position to extend still further its growing base in Wales. In fact, it is probably stronger in Wales today than at any time since the Protestant Reformation. Indeed, it may not be too fanciful to suggest that the Welsh, like their fellow Celts in Ireland, may yet be persuaded to pledge their allegiance to a universal Church, whose centre of power lies outside England and the British State, and return to the mainstream tradition of Western Christianity. The other 'winners' in the social and cultural climate of the new Wales are Churches in the evangelical tradition, some of them charismatic, some Pentecostal, who are making strenuous efforts to fill the spiritual vacuum created by the decline of traditional Welsh Nonconformity in what is an increasingly rootless society.

Signs of Hope

Is there then any hope that a Christian witness will survive or even revive in Wales, or are we left with a picture of unrelieved gloom and doom? I have already suggested that three traditions will certainly survive and that in two cases at least, namely the Roman Catholic Church and the new Churches of the conservative evangelical movement, grow stronger. But are there any positive signs of hope for new growth? My own strong impression is that there are, and so in the final part of this essay I want briefly to indicate where I see evidence that Christians in Wales can look to the new millennium with greater confidence than our analysis of the reasons for the decline in popularity of the institutional Churches might suggest. In particular, I want to explore four areas of growth : the assertion of life and of creation that has taken the place of the world-denying Puritanism of Welsh Nonconformity; the growing awareness of the 'spiritual' dimension of human experience; the significant expansion of a network of small groups of Christians, sometimes only loosely connected to the Churches, and finally the greater commitment of the 'remnant' of the faithful. Let us now consider each of these in turn.

We discussed earlier the almost universal rejection of puritanical attitudes to religion as reflected in the demise of the traditional Welsh 'Sabbath' and the abandonment of the 'Chapel' mentality. The flip side of that coin is a recovery of a world-affirming theology based in the main on a rediscovery of a theology of creation, largely generated by contemporary ecological and environmental awareness found in a wide variety of pressure-groups, who are by no means exclusively and in many cases not even predominantly Christian. The same sort of awareness of the essential goodness of creation characterizes the theological reflection of some feminist groups. Alongside this there is a reaffirmation of the incarnational principle of divine revelation, namely that God used human flesh as a vehicle for bringing the salvation of the whole created order into effect; this principle in turn undergirds the sacramental theology that characterizes a 'catholic' understanding of Christian theology, namely a belief that God is really present and apprehended in the material—traditionally in the elements of bread and wine. This again is in tune with the prevailing social concern of many, especially the young, for the environment and for showing a proper respect for planet (even Mother) Earth as God's creation. Such an ecological theology speaks to and for adherents of many faiths. In its extreme form it has led, even in Wales, to a revival of paganism or alternatively nature religion, which has filled a psychological, emotional and spiritual vacuum the institutional Churches have generally failed to recognize, let alone fill.

The same theological foundations undergird the activities of those Christians who have committed themselves, as Christians, to the struggle for social, political and economic justice, an aspect of Christian witness which is anathema to those who advocate or tacitly assent to the privatization of Christianity. As we have seen, privatizing religion is an integral part of the ideology of Thatcherite conservatism, which in this respect has taken to its logical conclusion the emphasis on the individual and on individual commitment that was central to the theology of the Protestant Reformers. Many Christians today are actively

36

engaged in the struggle for social justice, not just here in Wales, but all over the world. One could argue that, far from being seen as para-Church movements, bodies like Christian Aid, CAFOD and the Tear Fund should be seen as central to what it means to be the Church—the Church in action. Only thus can the Churches begin to recover the dynamic that is inherent in the gospel. And in this struggle Christians have found themselves standing shoulder to shoulder with others, who have long despaired of ever persuading the 'establishment' institutions we know as the Churches to act in the cause of the poor and oppressed.

Ecological concerns and the struggle for social justice have come to the top of the Christian agenda for some in the Churches and more perhaps outside the Churches in Wales. Similar trends can be seen in the composition of groups working for peace. This was particularly true in the 1970s and the 1980s, as the brave witness of the Greenham Common women illustrates. All this activity and the theological insights and emphases on which it is based—namely a recovery of the centrality of the doctrines of Creation and Incarnation, together with a growing realization that the role of the Church in society is to be a sacramental presence, an extension of the Incarnation—all this is a definite sign of hope for those who tend to despair at the decline of the 'old-style' Christian witness in Wales.

A second ground for hope stems from the findings of survey after survey into public attitudes to religious belief, which show overwhelming evidence of a residual belief in God (admittedly, under a number of different guises) among seventy to eighty per cent of the population. There is still, therefore, in spite of dwindling Church attendance, a widespread acceptance that there is a 'divine' or 'spiritual' dimension to life. This deep, maybe even subconscious, recognition of the existence of a power outside and beyond ourselves and our created order also accounts for the popularity of religious, almost invariably Christian, ceremonies to mark the so-called *rites de passage*, the big moments of life when the mystery of life is laid bare, particularly birth (baptisms), marriage (weddings) and death (funerals).

A similar deep-seated need to acknowledge and somehow respond to the spiritual, however that may be defined, probably lies at the root of two other recent developments, one directly related to Christian observance and the other a renewal of interest in a particular theology grounded in Welsh soil; I mean the popularity of charismatic-style worship, on the one hand, and the search for a distinctively Celtic Christianity and its theology and spirituality, on the other.

The modern charismatic movement, which is worldwide and which has affected all Christian traditions, has been widely welcomed and acclaimed as a genuine movement of the spirit, which has restored enthusiasm and life to the worship of many Churches. It has also given rise to a renewed interest in the ministry of healing—for example, through the laying-on of hands. In some respects charismatic worship reproduces many of the characteristic elements of the Welsh revivals, and especially of the Pentecostal movement that sprang from the 1904 revival. What it represents is a reaction against too much formalism and intellectualism in the Christian tradition by recovering the essentially emotional nature of worship and indeed by recognizing that the initial response of faith to the preaching of the gospel message comes from the heart rather than the head. Perhaps the most significant aspects of the movement are its worldwide appeal and its ability to transcend denominational boundaries. This suggests that it will prove more than an ephemeral phenomenon, and that it will have a lasting effect on the worship and pastoral outreach of all Christian denominations. In that sense, it is a sign of hope and a manifestation of the power of the spirit to breathe new life into dead Churches.

Our other development is at the same time both intellectual and emotional in the sense that it is a response to an emotional and psychological need on the part of a growing number of Christians in Wales to re-establish their roots in the Celtic Church, which were so tragically and thoroughly severed at the time of the Protestant Reformation. This 'movement' is not simply a romantic quest for a mythological past, nor is it attempting to return to the medieval Catholicism that Saunders Lewis championed earlier in the century. It is rather an honest academic endeavour involving serious research to reconstruct a theology and a spirituality and maybe even a practice that was distinctively Celtic, a form of Christianity that was developed by the Celtic peoples of Ireland and Wales in particular. This Christianity was both catholic in the sense that it had strong links with the rest of worldwide Christianity at that time, and peculiarly Celtic in that it reflected the aspirations and experiences of the Celtic peoples on both sides of the Irish Sea.

No one can travel far in Wales without being aware of the *llannau* and the Celtic saints whose names they bear. The history of many of the *llannau* and of their saints is lost in the mists of time; nonetheless, the *llannau* and their saints are the most distinctive part of our heritage as Christians in Wales. Too often over the past two centuries and a half the impression has been given that the true faith started in Wales with the Protestant Reformation. Even the Church in Wales, which is privileged for various historical reasons to have almost all the *llannau*, has with a few honourable exceptions in the last century and in this tended to ignore its Celtic roots or else to misuse the evidence to promote the empire-building ambitions of some of its bishops. The balance is now on the way to being redressed, thanks to the efforts of scholars like Patrick Thomas, A.M. Allchin and Oliver Davies, aided and abetted by the scholarly and saintly Bishop Rowan of Monmouth. It may not be a coincidence that these same scholars have an active interest in Eastern Orthodox Christianity, a form of Christianity that historical evidence suggests exerted some influence on the development of Celtic Christianity. This is not the place to engage in that particular historical debate, nor am I qualified to do so. What is relevant for us is that growing awareness of our past and of our ancient Christian heritage that reaches back over 1500 years or more is a real sign of hope and confidence in the future of Christianity in Wales. It is also likely that greater knowledge and awareness of the kind of Christianity espoused by our Celtic ancestors of the first millennium will eventually influence both the belief and the practice of Christians in Wales in the third millennium of the Christian era.

The growth of grassroots communities of committed

Christians (sometimes called base ecclesial communities) in countries around the world has been one of the most remarkable signs of hope and renewal in the Christian Church over the past quarter of a century. The movement began in the Roman Catholic Church in Latin America, where it gained considerable momentum after Vatican II, as a response to illiteracy and ignorance among the poor and deprived. The primary purpose of this movement was to 'conscientize' the poor through education, i.e. to raise awareness among the poor of the reasons for their poverty, and thus to convince them that they could do something about it.

Typically a group or community will have around twelve members, sometimes as few as six, sometimes as many as twenty. They meet regularly (usually weekly) to reflect on their experience critically in the light of Scripture and of Christian, i.e. Catholic, teaching and this in turn leads to critical reflection on the Bible and tradition in the light of their experience of the liberation struggle. These Latin American communities, which are predominantly lay, are the best-known examples of this worldwide movement, but there are many others in all parts of the world and across many different Christian traditions. For example, much of the pressure for change in the political system in Eastern Europe in the late 1980s came from grassroots Christian groups, who challenged the hierarchy of their Churches to stand up and be counted.

Britain and Ireland have also experienced a remarkable growth of such groups, though they are far from uniform either in their composition or in the way they operate. There are, however, fewer groups in Wales than in other parts of the British Isles, though Wales too is now seeing the development of a network of groups devoted to prayer or Bible study and reflection across the denominational spectrum. Some of these groups have particular interests of a 'political' kind, such as peace, justice or the environment, which they see as an essential element in Christian witness. This concentration on 'awareness-raising' group activity is also one of the major contributions to Christian growth in Wales of the pioneering feminist theology movement.

My own feeling is that, as in other continents, so too in Wales the future health of the Christian Church and its witness lies as much with these groups as with the mainline Churches. There are similarities between this development and the longer established house Church movement, many of whose members have turned their backs on the institutional Church, but not on Christ. For such people worship as well as practical outreach is centred on the life of the small group. As in other countries, so too in Wales, the grassroots movement is largely lay; its leadership is as likely to be female as male, in contrast to the male-dominated hierarchies of the mainline Churches. Furthermore, the degree of commitment to the gospel among the membership is often deeper than that found in the mainline Churches.

One of the major advantages of this movement is that these Christians, unlike those who are still part of the institutional Church, are not encumbered by the financial burden of maintaining unsuitable, but expensive plant, or with the equally costly responsibility of supporting a professional ministry. In this sense they show a realism which has often eluded the institutional Churches. This releases their energy to focus not only on the practical expression of their Christian commitment (e.g. campaigning for peace and justice), but on the spiritual dimension of faith as well (e.g. prayer and meditation). They often claim, and it is hard to contest their claim, that they are recreating the kinds of communities that characterized the early Christian movement in the first century or so of its existence, and that consequently they are nearer to living out the Christian gospel in the way that Jesus intended. Time alone will tell whether or not these claims are exaggerated; in the mean time, the establishment of this diffuse network of small grassroots communities of committed Christians, sometimes only very loosely connected to the institutional Churches, may be regarded as a definite sign of hope and renewal in Wales, as in the rest of the Christian world.

The starting-point of this discussion of Christianity in Wales today was the decline in popularity of the institutional Churches, and especially the Free Churches, a decline that can be demonstrated statistically as well as experienced subjectively. One aspect of this decline, however, is a sign of hope, namely the determination and depth of commitment of the remnant. I have argued that, with the exception of the Roman Catholic Church and some congregations in the charismatic and evangelical traditions, the numerical decline of the mainline Churches is likely to continue, and that traditional Welsh Nonconformity will all but disappear. Having said that, I have predicted that Christian witness in other forms will continue and probably grow stronger. We are likely to see smaller congregations, but their members will be deeply committed Christians.

Church membership is no longer regarded as an essential qualification for social respectability. We even come across Welsh-speaking atheists and agnostics now, who have no qualms in acknowledging their lack of religious belief openly. Respectability is no longer a necessary characteristic of being Christian either, and this means that much of the cant and hypocrisy of yesteryear has gone. All this is good and healthy; it is a clear sign of hope for the future. The Churches may become marginalized; they will certainly be a minority cause, but this may in the end enable them to rediscover their true role in society. If the Churches are to be true witnesses of the gospel of Jesus Christ they can hardly expect to be popular. As history shows, there is more than an element of truth in what appears to be a very hard saying that the blood of the martyrs is the seed of the Church. Marginalization is in some respects a modern form of martyrdom, and since this is the fate of most Churches in Wales their decline in popularity may paradoxically be a sign of hope for the future.

I was born into the Church and nurtured in the Church. Most of what I am and have I owe to the Church, but like many children in the everyday world I have a love-hate relationship with Mother Church. It grieves me that the Church I love should be in decline, but it irritates and exasperates me to the point of despair that many in the Church refuse to read the signs of the times and are content, ostrich-like, to bury their heads in the comfortable sand of the status quo, though such comfort as this affords is likely to be short-lived. Again, like many Welsh people, I am torn between the comfort of conservatism and its resistance to and fear of change, on the one hand, and the challenge of

42

radicalism and its openness to the future, on the other. At this juncture in our national history and in the history of Christianity in our land what is required of Christians in Wales is the boldness and courage to be truly radical—to go back to our roots, not only to our roots in the Celtic Church, but to our original roots in the small communities of enthusiastic and committed Christians who first responded to the call of the gospel in countries around the Mediterranean Sea. If we can recover these roots and draw on the strength and inspiration they give we can face the new millennium not with despair, but in hope, the hope that we shall be worthy servants of society in this dear land of Wales.

changing **WALES**

GW00730009

| TALK |

Arabic

JONATHAN FEATHERSTONE

Series Editor: Alwena Lamping

The author would like to dedicate this book to Angela.

Published by BBC Active, an imprint of Educational Publishers LLP, part of the Pearson Education Group, Edinburgh Gate, Harlow, Essex CM20 2JE, England.

© Educational Publishers LLP 2015

BBC logo © BBC 1996. BBC and BBC ACTIVE are trademarks of the British Broadcasting Corporation.

First published 2009
Second edition 2015

5 4 3

The right of Jonathan Featherstone to be identified as author of this Work has been asserted by him in accordance with the Copyright, Designs and Patents Act, 1988.

ISBN 978-1-4066-8005-8

Cover design: Two Associates
Cover photograph: © iStock.com/saras66
Insides design: Nicolle Thomas, Rob Lian
Layout: DTP Media Ltd. www.dtp-media.co.uk
Arabic layout: Samar Maakaron
Illustrations © Mark Duffin
Publisher: Debbie Marshall
Development manager: Tara Dempsey
Development editor: Nadira Auty
Project editor: Emma Brown

Audio producer: Colette Thomson, Footstep Productions Ltd.
Sound engineer: Andrew Garratt
Presenters: Alia Al Zougby, Amal Jazaerli, Nayef Rashed, Radwan Sammak

Printed and bound in China. (CTPSC/03)

The Publisher's policy is to use paper manufactured from sustainable forests.

Contents

Introduction

Welcome to **Talk Arabic**, BBC Active's new course for absolute beginners. It consists of a book and two 60-minute CDs recorded by native Arabic speakers.

Designed for adults, learning at home or in a class, **Talk Arabic** is the ideal introduction to Arabic, covering the basic everyday language for a visit to an Arabic-speaking country, whether for work or on holiday. It is suitable for a first level qualification, such as the Breakthrough level of the national Languages Ladder.

Modern Standard Arabic (MSA), which is the formal language of the broadcast media, the press and literature, is not used for everyday informal conversations and transactions. **Talk Arabic** has therefore chosen to focus on the Arabic of the Levant, spoken in Lebanon, Syria, Jordan and Palestine and widely understood elsewhere. It is not too far removed from MSA, and some of the main differences are highlighted on pages 99-100.

A great advantage of learning Levantine Arabic is that it can be learnt to a reasonable level without having to master the complex Arabic script. To enable you to make faster progress in speaking Arabic, **Talk Arabic** presents the sounds of Arabic using the script used for English and other Western languages (known as Roman script). The basics of Arabic script are also introduced within self-contained sections of the book.

Talk Arabic encourages you to make genuine progress and promotes a real sense of achievement. The key to its effectiveness lies in its systematic approach. Key features include:

- simple step-by-step presentation of new language
- involvement and interaction at every stage of the learning process
- useful language learning strategies
- regular progress checks
- reference section, including guide to pronunciation, grammar summary, audio transcripts and glossary

Acknowledgements

BBC Active would like to thank everyone who contributed to this course. Our particular thanks go to Leslie McLoughlin of Exeter University and Ruba Jurdi Associates.

How to use Talk Arabic

Wherever you see this: **1•5**, the phrases or dialogues are recorded on the CD (i.e. CD1, track 5).

Each of the 10 units is completed in 10 easy-to-follow steps.

1   Read the first page of the unit to focus on what you're aiming to learn and to set your learning in context. Then follow steps 2 to 5 for each of the next four pages of the unit.

2   Listen to the key words and phrases – don't be tempted to read them first. Then listen to them again, this time reading them in your book too. Finally, try reading them out loud before listening one more time.

3   Work your way, step by step, through the activities. These highlight key language elements and are carefully designed to develop your listening skills and your understanding of Arabic. You can check your answers in *Transcripts and answers* starting on page 113.

4   Read the **bil 9arabi** explanations of how Arabic works as you come to them. Wherever you see **G00** these are developed further in the *Grammar* section at the back of the book.

5   After completing the activities, close your book and listen to the conversations straight through. The more times you listen, the more familiar and comfortable you'll become with the sounds of Arabic. You might also like to read the transcripts at this stage.

6   Complete the consolidation activities on the *Put it all together* page, checking your answers with the *Transcripts and answers*.

7   Use the language you've just learnt. The audio presenters will prompt you and guide you through the *Now you're talking!* page as you practise speaking Arabic.

8   Check your progress. First, test your knowledge with the *quiz*. Then check whether you can do everything on the *checklist* – if in doubt, go back and spend some more time on the relevant section. You'll have further opportunities to check your progress in the strategic *Checkpoints* after units 4, 7 and 10.

9   Read the learning strategy at the end of the unit, which provides ideas for consolidating and extending what you've learnt.

10 Finally, relax and listen to the whole unit, understanding what the people are saying in Arabic and taking part in the conversations. This time you may not need to have the book to hand.

Pronunciation guide

Talk Arabic presents the sounds of Levantine Arabic using Roman script, i.e. the same script as English. This is called transliteration. In Arabic script capital letters aren't used for places, and so the transliteration will reflect the actual sounds e.g. **bayruut** *Beirut*, **Halab** *Aleppo*. It does, however, show all names with initial capitals in order to distinguish them from general vocabulary e.g. **Mona**, **Zeinab**, **Sami**.

Vowels
The vowel sounds are represented as:

a	i	u	aa	ii	uu	aw	ay
c<u>a</u>t	b<u>i</u>n	p<u>u</u>t	c<u>ar</u>	b<u>ee</u>n	p<u>oo</u>l	c<u>ow</u>	d<u>a</u>y

Consonants
Many consonants sound much as they do in English but there are a few extra sounds in Arabic:

- The capital letters **D**, **DH**, **S**, **T** are used to show 'heavier' versions of **d**, **dh**, **s**, **t**. Listen out for them on the audio to hear exactly how they're pronounced. **H** is a breathy **h** as if breathing on glasses to clean them.

  r is more rolled than in English

  gh sounds like a French r, or a gargling sound

  j sounds like the soft s of lei<u>s</u>ure

  kh sounds like the ch of Lo<u>ch</u> Ness

  q and **'** have two sounds: either the hard ck in knu<u>ck</u>le or the cockney glottal stop in bu'er (butter)

  9 is used because there's no English equivalent of the sound it represents, which is similar to a strangled ah sound made by narrowing the throat.

- Where the transliteration shows a double consonant these must both be pronounced to give a long sound, such as **sayyaara** *car*, which is pronounced **say-yaara**.

- There is no v or p sound. As a rule they become **b**, e.g. **suubermarket**.

Stress
Most Arabic words are stressed, and this varies from dialect to dialect. Generally it falls on the last but one syllable in a word:

shuu <u>is</u>mak? *What's your name?*   **wayn <u>saa</u>kin?** *Where do you live?*

ahlan wa sahlan

saying hello

... and goodbye

introducing yourself

... and getting to know people

In Arabic-speaking countries greetings and social pleasantries are very important and a wide variety exist. Most greetings have a set reply, so it's useful to learn each greeting as a pair. If someone says **marHaba** *hello*, for example, the response is **marHabtayn** literally *two hellos*.

Alongside **marHaba** the most widely used greetings are **is-salaam 9alaykum** *may peace be upon you*, **ahlan wa sahlan** *hello*, and **ahlan** *hi*.

is-salaam 9alaykum is a little more formal and often heard when one person greets a number of people at the same time. **ahlan wa sahlan** means *welcome* as well as *hello*, and is used in particular when someone welcomes you into their home.

Greetings and welcomes will be repeated several times throughout an initial conversation, the more times the better.

Saying hello

1   1•2 Listen to the key language:

is-salaam 9alaykum.	May peace be upon you.
wa 9alaykum is-salaam.	*reply*: And upon you be peace.
ahlan wa sahlan.	Hello./Welcome.
ahlan fiik/ahlan fiiki.	*reply*: Hello. (to m/f)
ahlan.	Hi./Hello.
kiif il-Haal?	How are you?
bi-khayr, shukran.	Well, thank you.
il-Hamdullilaah.	Praise be to God.
w-inta/w-inti?	And you? (to m/f)

2   1•3 Listen as Hiba Mustafa, the receptionist at the Umayyad Hotel greets people. Which greetings does she use?

bil 9arabi In Arabic …

when you greet someone you know well, you can use **ya** in front of their name:

ahlan ya Ahmad. *Hi Ahmad*. ahlan ya Mona. *Hi Mona*.

In a more formal setting, such as at work or in a hotel, you can use **ya** with someone's title:

is-salaam 9alaykum ya madaam Fawziyya/ya sayyid Salih/ya aanisa Hoda. *Hello Mrs Fawziyya/Mr Salih/Miss Hoda*.

3   1•4 Later Mr Hamdi meets Mrs Fawziyya in the hotel lobby. Tick the key phrases above in the order which you hear them.

4   1•5 Listen as two friends greet each other:
- How does Muhsin greet Mona? Ehlen ya Mona kiif il-Haal?
- How does Mona reply? bikhayr shukran, wa inta?

... and goodbye

1   1•6 Listen to the key language:

SabaaH il-khayr.	Good morning.
SabaaH in-nuur.	*reply*: Good morning.
masaa il-khayr.	Good evening.
masaa in-nuur.	*reply*: Good evening.
ma9a as-salaama.	Goodbye.
allaah yisalmak/yisalmik.	*reply*: Goodbye. (to m/f) *Lit*. May God bless you.
ashuufak/ashuufik ba9dayn.	See you later. (to m/f)

2   1•7 Listen to Hiba Mustafa saying hello and goodbye to the following guests at the Umayyad Hotel and match them with the above phrases.

Mrs Fawziyya .....*SabaaH il-khayr*.....   Miss Hoda ....*masaa in-nuur*....

Mr Hamdi ....*SabaaH il-khayr*....   Mr Haddad ....*ma9a as-salaama*....

ma9a as-salaama

---

bil 9arabi In Arabic ...

the words for *you* in sentences like *God bless you* or *See you later* are **-ak** for a man and **-ik** for a woman. They go at the end of the verb:

ashuuf<u>ak</u>. *See <u>you</u>.* (m)   **allaah yisalm<u>ak</u>.** *God bless <u>you</u>.* (m)

ashuuf<u>ik</u>. *See <u>you</u>.* (f)   **allaah yisalm<u>ik</u>.** *God bless <u>you</u>.* (f)

---

3   1•8 Listen to Mrs Fawziyya talking to some people. Circle m if she's talking to a man or f for a woman. You will hear **kiif Haalak?** which is another way of saying *How are you?*

1   **m**   f   2   **m**   f   3   **m**   f   4   **m**   f   5   **m**   f

4   Now try the following. How would you:

- say *good morning* to your friend Rania?   *SabaaH il-khayr ya Rania*
- reply when a man says goodbye to you?   *Allah yisalmak*
- say *see you later* to a female colleague?   *ashuufik ba9dayn*

Introducing yourself

1 1•9 Listen to the key language:

ana ...	I am ...
inta/inti ...?	Are you ...? (to m/f) *informal*
HaDirtak/HaDirtik ...?	Are you ...? (to m/f) *formal*
aywa, ana ...	Yes, I am ...
laa', ana mish ...	No, I'm not ...
law samaHt/law samaHti.	Excuse me. (to m/f)

2 1•10 Mona is waiting for Muhsin's colleagues to show up. She hasn't met them before. Listen and tick the four people she's looking for.

Jamal   Lutfi   Nureddine   Mustafa   Zeinab   Samia

---

bil 9arabi In Arabic ...

there are no words for *am*, *is*, *are* – if you want to say *I am*, *you are*, *he is* etc. you just use *I*, *you*, *he*, etc. on their own:

ana *I/I am*

inta *you/you are* (m)   inti *you/you are* (f)
huwwa *he/he is*   hiyya *she/she is*

ana Mona *I'm Mona*; huwwa Jamal *He's Jamal*; hiyya Farida *She's Farida*.

In simple spoken sentences like these, *not* is **mish**:
ana mish Mona *I'm not Mona*.

G8

---

3 1•11 A number of delegates are checking in at a conference in Cairo and introducing themselves. Listen and fill in the gaps:

- .... **HaDirtak Mustafa Amin?**
- .... **ana Mustafa Amin, wa ....?**
- **ana Adnan Hasan.**
- **ahlan wa sahlan.** .... **Mustafa Amin.** .... **Dalia Mustafa?**
- **laa',** .... **Dalia Mustafa, ana Amira Ahmad!**
- **ahlan, ya Amira!**

... and getting to know people

1 **1•12** Listen to the key language:

shuu ismak/ismik?   What's your name? (to m/f)
ismi ...   My name is …
tasharrafna.   Pleased to meet you. *Lit*. We have been honoured.
ish-sharaf ili.   *reply*: The pleasure is mine. *Lit*. The honour is mine.

---

bil 9arabi In Arabic …

to say *my*, you add -i to the noun you're talking about: **ism** *name*, **ismi** *my name*.

To say *your*, you add -ak or -ik: **ismak** *your name* (m), **ismik** *your name* (f).

G5

---

2 **1•13** There's a wedding reception at the Hotel Umayyad. Listen to a conversation between Sami Suleiman and Nadia Rif'at and tick these phrases as you hear them. Which phrase is left over?

ismi ...	✓	**ahlan fiik.**	✓
ish-sharaf ili.	✓	**shuu ismik?**	✓
shuu ismak?		**tasharrafna.**	✓

3 **1•14** At the Umayyad Hotel bar guests are finding out each other's names. Listen and complete the first part of the conversation:

- **ahlan wa sahlan.** *shw ismik* ....?
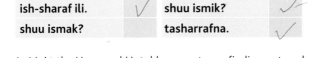
- *ismi.* **Zeinab,** *no inty* ....?
- **ismi Ahmad,** *tashavrafn . shuu ismal* ....?

4 **1•15** Sami is introduced to some more people. Listen and number the replies in the order he says them.

a **marHabtayn, shuu ismik?** *2*
b **bi-khayr il-Hamdullilaah.** *4*
c **ahlan fiik, ismi Sami.** *1*
d **ish-sharaf ili. w-inta shuu ismak?** *3*

put it all together

1 Match the English with the Arabic phrases:

a	How are you? 7	①	tasharrafna.
b	Pleased to meet you. 1	②	ashuufak ba9dayn.
c	May peace be upon you. 8	③	marHabtayn.
d	Good evening. (reply) 5	④	SabaaH il-khayr.
e	Well, thank you. 9	⑤	masaa in-nuur.
f	Hello. (reply) 3	⑥	ahlan wa sahlan.
g	Hello. (welcome) 6	⑦	kiif il-Haal?
h	See you later. (to m) 2	⑧	is-salaam 9alaykum.
i	Good morning. 4	⑨	bi-khayr shukran.

2 What could these people be saying to each other?

a

SabaaH il-khayr
SabaaH in-nuur

b

masaa il-kheyr
masaa in-nuur

c

is-salaam wa 9alaykum
wa 9alaykum is-salaam

d

ashuufik ba9dayn / masa aj-salam
ashuufak ba9dayn / allah jiGalmik
allah jiGal mik

3 How would you ....

a say *hi* to your friend, Ahmad?

b reply to a man who greeted you with **ahlan wa sahlan**?

c ask Farida *and you, how are you?*

a) ehlen ya Ahmad
b) ehlen fiik
c) wa inti, kiif il-Haal

now you're talking!

1 **1•16** Answer as if you were Barbara Cox, on holiday in Damascus. A fellow guest greets you in the hotel lobby.

- **masaa il-khayr.**
- ◆ Greet him appropriately. *masaa in-nuur*
- **ahlan wa sahlan, ana ismi Nabiil. shuu ismik?**
- ◆ Reply to the greeting, and introduce yourself. *ahlan fiik, ana ismi Barbra*
- **tasharrafna.**
- ◆ Reply accordingly. *ish-sharaf ili*

2 **1•17** Nabiil introduces you to his wife. *tasharrafna, kiif il-Haal?*

- ◆ Say that you're pleased to meet her and ask her how she is.
- **bi-khayr, shukran. il-Hamdullilaah. wa HaDirtik?**
- ◆ Say you're well, thank you. *bi khayr, shukran*
- **ma9a as-salaama. ashuufik ba9dayn.**
- ◆ Reply accordingly. *allah yisalmik ashuufik ba9dayn*

3 **1•18** The next morning you meet a friend, Jamal. You think you recognise his friend Mustafa.

- ◆ Greet him. *ahlan wa sahlan*
- **ahlan fiiki, ya Barbara.**
- ◆ Say hi to his friend, and ask if he is Mustafa. *ehlen, HaDitak Mstfa?*
- **laa', ana mish Mustafa, ismi Mourad!**

quiz

1 When do you say **wa 9alaykum is-salaam**? *As a reply to is-salaam 9alaykum*
2 How do you address a woman formally as *you*? *HaDirtik*
3 What's the difference between **law samaHt** and **law SamaHti**? *f* *m*
4 Would you use **SabaaH il-khayr** in the morning or the evening?
5 Can you think of three ways of saying *hello*? *is-salaam 9alaykum* *ehlen wa sehlen* *ehlen*
6 How do you ask a man his name? *shuu ismak?*
7 What is the correct reply to **tasharrafna**? *ish-sharaf ili*
8 If tomorrow is **bukra**, how do you say *see you tomorrow* to a male friend? *ashuufak bukra*

Now check whether you can ...

- greet someone and respond to their greeting
- ask how they are and tell them how you are
- say good morning, afternoon and evening
- introduce yourself and reply to introductions
- say who you are and ask someone their name
- say goodbye

The best way of developing good Arabic pronunciation is by listening to the audio as often as you can and repeating things out loud, imitating the speakers as closely as you can. It really does make a difference since it familiarises you with the sounds of Arabic and in particular gets you used to those sounds which don't exist in English.

Arabic script: introduction

Arabic is a Semitic language which is read from right to left. It has an alphabet of 28 letters, 14 of which are sun letters and 14 moon letters. Whether a word starts with a sun or moon letter affects the way it sounds when accompanied by **il** *the*. Nouns which start with a moon letter keep the **il** as in: **il-maghrib** *Morocco*, **il-urdun** *Jordan*, whereas nouns which start with a sun letter, replace the **-l** in **il** by that letter: **is-sa9uudiyya** *Saudi Arabia*. This only applies to what is said or read aloud. The **il** always appears in the written form. In MSA (see page 99) *the* is **al** and this is how you'll see it in the script sections. The full alphabet is shown on the next page and, in addition, the letters are introduced in small groups at regular points in the book.

Arabic doesn't use capital letters but some of the letters look different depending on whether they're written on their own or at the beginning, middle or end of a word. Despite the differences, each letter has an essential characteristic which it keeps wherever it occurs.

Arabic letters are intricate, and you'll see that some have similar shapes but vary according to how many dots they have above or below them. Many of the letters join onto each other, most from both right and left. There are many different styles of Arabic script, and Arabic calligraphy is a central feature in Islamic art, with letters and words put together to form superb patterns and shapes.

Reading Arabic script

You don't normally see short vowels (**a**, **i**, **u**) written within words appearing on everyday signs or in newspapers and books, so it's important that you get used to reading without them:
bayt *house* is written **b-y-t** بيت
maktab *office* is written **m-k-t-b** مكتب

The long vowels are represented using the letters, alif ا (**aa**), yaa ي (**ii**) and waw و (**uu**):
maTaar *airport* is written **m-T-aa-r** مطار
mudiir *manager* is written **m-d-ii-r** مدير

There are conventions for representing vowels at the beginning and end of words, which will be introduced as you work through the sections.

When a consonant is doubled in Arabic the letter is only written once. A marker called a 'shadda' ّ can be placed above the letter to show it is doubled, but you won't often see it written in: **jadda** جدّة *Jeddah*.

Isolated letter	Name	Sound	Example		Sun/moon letter
ا	alif	*see below*	باب	baab	☽
ب	baa	b	بيت	bayt	☽
ت	taa	t	تلفون	tilifawn	☀
ث	thaa	th	إثنين	ithnayn	☀
ج	jiim	j	جميل	jamiil	☽
ح	Haa	H	أحمد	aHmad	☽
خ	khaa	kh	أخي	akhi	☽
د	daal	d	مدرسة	madrasa	☀
ذ	dhaal	dh	لذيذ	ladhiidh	☀
ر	raa	r	سيارة	sayyaara	☀
ز	zaa	z	زميل	zamiil	☀
س	siin	s	سوق	suuq	☀
ش	shiin	sh	شمس	shams	☀
ص	Saad	S	مصر	maSr	☀
ض	Daad	D	الرياض	ar-riyaaD	☀
ط	Taa	T	طالب	Taalib	☀
ظ	DHaa	DH	ظهر	DHuhr	☀
ع	9ayn	9	عندي	9andi	☽
غ	ghayn	gh	غالي	ghaali	☽
ف	faa	f	فندق	funduq	☽
ق	qaaf	q or '	القاهرة	al-qaahira	☽
			مقاس	ma'aas	
ك	kaaf	k	كتاب	kitaab	☽
ل	laam	l	لون	lawn	☀
م	miim	m	مدير	mudiir	☽
ن	nuun	n	نور	nuur	☀
ه	haa	h	هو	huwwa	☽
و	waw	w, uu	ولد	walad	☽
ي	yaa	y, ii	يوم	yawm	☽

alif can represent the sound of the long vowel **aa**, and at the beginning of words the short vowels **a**, **i**, **u** (with the hamza, see page 68).

min wayn inta?

talking about where you're from

... and your nationality

saying where you live

giving your phone number

In the Arab world people are always curious to know which country foreign visitors are from and it may be one of the first things you're asked.

The names of most Western countries don't sound very different in Arabic; for example, **hulanda** is *Holland*, **iskutlanda** *Scotland*, **irlanda** *Ireland* and **amriika** *America*.

Certain Arab countries have the word **il** *the* within their name. For example you will hear **maSr** and **lubnaan** for *Egypt* and *Lebanon* but **il-maghrib** and **il-urdun** for *Morocco* and *Jordan*. This is also true for Arabic cities, **baghdaad** is *Baghdad*, **ir-riyaaD** *Riyadh*, and **id-daar il-bayDa** *Casablanca*. **il-jazaa'ir** can mean *Algeria* or *Algiers*.

Talking about where you're from

1 **1•19** Listen to the key language:

min wayn inta/inti?	Where are you from? (to m/f)
ana min briiTaanya.	I'm from Britain.
inta/inti min is-sa9uudiyya?	Are you from Saudi Arabia? (to m/f)
laa', ana min il-maghrib.	No, I'm from Morocco.
ana min il-qaahira kamaan.	I'm from Cairo as well.

here n

---

bil 9arabi ...

the word for *the* is **il**, although the way it appears changes depending on the first letter of the following noun. Of the 28 letters in the Arabic alphabet, 14 are called sun letters and 14 are moon letters. Nouns which start with a moon letter take **il-**: **il-maghrib** *Morocco*. But if a noun starts with a sun letter, the **l** in **il-** is replaced by that letter: **is-sa9uudiyya** *Saudi Arabia*. (Refer to page 16 for the full list of sun and moon letters.)

---

2 **1•20** Farida Haddad is running an Arabic language school in Beirut. She asks her new teachers where they're from. Listen and tick which country each one is from. *are mish min ---*

huwa
hiyya

	is-sa9uudiyya *Saudi Arabia*	**lubnaan** *Lebanon*	**suuriya** *Syria*	**maSr** *Egypt*	**il-urdun** *Jordan*
George		✓			
Muhsin				✓	
Tareq	✓				
Nadia					✓
Ruba			✓		

3 **1•21** Mark Jones is attending a conference in Damascus and asks a fellow delegate which city he comes from. Circle the correct answer:

Taraablus *Tripoli*   **jadda** *Jeddah*   (**iskandariyya**) *Alexandria*

4 How would you ask Farida where she's from?
min wayn inti ya Farida?

... and your nationality

1   **1•22** Listen to the key language:

inta briiTaani?	Are you British? (to m)
inti briiTaaniyya?	Are you British? (to f)
aywa, ana briiTaani/briiTaaniyya.	Yes, I am British. (m/f)
laa', ana mish lubnaani/lubnaaniyya.	No, I'm not Lebanese. (m/f)

(mush + you region)

---

bil 9arabi ...

you change the ending of the name of a country to get the
nationality. The nationality ending for a male is **-i**, while the
feminine ending is **-iyya**:

briiTaanya *Britain*	**briiTaani** (m)	**briiTaaniyya** (f) *British*
lubnaan *Lebanon*	**lubnaani** (m)	**lubnaaniyya** (f) *Lebanese*

G7

---

2   **1•23** Match the **jinsiyya** *nationality* to the **balad** *country*, then give
the feminine forms. Try saying them out loud, then listen to check.

suuri   maSri   ingliizi   iskutlandi   maghribi

sa9uudi   fransi   tuunisi   irlandi   honnot

amriika *America*	amriiki/amriikiyya
iskutlanda *Scotland*	iskutlandi / iskutlandiyya
fransa *France*	fransi / fransiyya
ingilterra *England*	ingliizi / ingliiziyya
irlanda *Ireland*	irlandi / irlandiyya
maSr *Egypt*	maSri / masriyya
il-maghrib *Morocco*	maghribi / maghribiyya
is-sa9uudiyya *Saudi Arabia*	sa9uudi / sa9uudiyya
tuunis *Tunisia*	tuunisi / tuunisiyya
suuriya *Syria*	suuri / suuriyya

---

3   **1•24** The students at Farida's school are getting to know each other.
Circle the correct answers to describe their nationalities:

Hussein: **maSri/lubnaani**   Maha: **maghribiyya/lubnaaniyya**
Adam: **irlandi/amriiki**   Jacqueline: **fransiyya/suuriyya**
David: **ingliizi/iskutlandi**

Saying where you live

1 **1•25** Listen to the key language:

wayn saakin/saakna?	Where do you live? (to m/f)
ana saakin fi dimashq.	I live in Damascus. (m)
ana saakna fi iskandariyya.	I live in Alexandria. (f)
ana mish saakin/saakna fi Halab.	I don't live in Aleppo. (m/f)
inta saakin/inti saakna fil-qaahira?	Do you live in Cairo? (to m/f)

fi+il fi)

---

bil 9arabi ...

the key word when talking about where you live is saakin. It has three different forms, depending on who's talking or being talked about:

- one male saakin: (ana/inta/huwwa) saakin *I/you/he live(s)*
- one female saakna: (ana/inti/hiyya) saakna *I/you/she live(s)*
- more than one person saakniin

Not is mish: huwwa mish saakin he doesn't live

In grammar terms saakin is an active participle, and you'll come across more words that work in the same way.   **G12**

---

2 **1•26** Farida asks some of her new Arabic teachers where they live in their home countries. Listen to their conversation and complete the dialogue below.

- wayn .... fil-urdun, ya Nadia?
- ana saakna .fi. 9ammaan.
- w-inta ya Muhsin, ... saakin?
- ana saakin fil-qaahira
- inta saakin fil-qaahira kamaan, ya George?
- laa', ana mish saakin fil-qaahira, ana saakin fi bayruut.

3 **1•27** At the conference Mark Jones is telling Hasan Shoukry where the other delegates live. Listen and match each person with their city. You'll hear **bass** *but.*

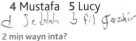

1 Adnan 2 Amira 3 Hussein
4 Mustafa 5 Lucy

[handwritten at top: 6-9-1-3-5-8-0-2-10-4, with 7 below the 1]

Giving your phone number

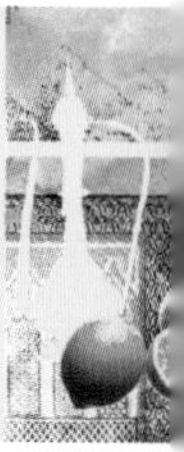

1 **1•28** Listen to the numbers from 0–10:

0	**Sifr**	4	**arba9a**	8	**tamanya** *[handwritten: tmanya]*
1	**waaHid**	5	**khamsa**	9	**tis9a**
2	**itnayn**	6	**sitta**	10	**9ashara**
3	**talaata**	7	**sab9a**		

2 **1•29** Listen and jot down the numbers you hear. *[handwritten: 6 – 9 – 1 – 3 – 5 – 8 – 0 – 2 10 – 4 – 7]*

[handwritten: (raqmal nowl lor l)]

3 **1•30** Now listen to these phrases relating to **raqm it-tilifawn** *the telephone number* *[handwritten: (raqmal tilefona l)]*

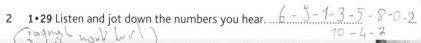

shuu raqm tilifawnak/ *[handwritten: my]*	What's your telephone number?
tilifawnik?	(to m/f)
raqm tilifawn il-bayt ... *[handwritten: (ij)]*	My home telephone number (is) ...
raqm il-mubayl ...	The mobile number (is) ...
raqm tilifawn il-maktab ... *[handwritten: ohi]*	The telephone number of the office (is) ...

[handwritten left margin: obl (Hawl) own]
[handwritten: raqm bayt;]

4 **1•31** Ayman wants to make a note of Hasan's phone numbers at the Cairo conference. See if you can figure out which number is for home, office and mobile. You'll hear **wi** as an alternative to **wa** *and*.

0134 0460 *[handwritten: maktab]*   0993 2271 *[handwritten: mubayl]*   0146 0179 *[handwritten: bayt]*

5 **1•32** Farida is on a business trip to London and gives her contact details to a colleague. Try saying her office telephone number before you listen and then make a note of her home and mobile numbers.

raqm tilifawn il-maktab 0144 2776
raqm tilifawn il-bayt *[handwritten: 0144 1665]*   *[handwritten: 0144 18615]*
raqm il-mubayl *[handwritten: 0934 2752]*   *[handwritten: 0934 77 92]*

---

bil 9arabi ...

when two or more nouns such as *phone number* are used together you only use **il-** *the* on the final noun: **raqm it-tilifawn** *the telephone number* lit. *number the telephone*; **raqm tilifawn il-maktab** *the office telephone number* lit. *number telephone the office*.   **G6**

put it **all together**

1 How would the following people say where they're from and what their nationality is?

Example: Leila - Amman, Jordan
ana min il-urdun, saakna fi 9ammaan. ana urduniyya.

a Ahmad – Cairo, Egypt *ana min masr, ana saakin fil qahira-ana misri*
b Amina – Casablanca, Morocco *ana min l-maghrib, ana saakna fi id-daar l bayda*
c Zubayr – Jeddah, Saudi Arabia *ana min il-saudiyya, ana saakin fi Jedda, ana maghrabi? saudi*
d Latifa – Damascus, Syria *ana min surie ana saakna fi dimashq. ana suriyya*
e Ewan – Edinburgh, Scotland *ana min isktlanda ana saakin fi Edinbrah. ana skotlac*

2 Complete the following in words and figures:

a **tamanya + waaHid** = ...tis'a.....
b **sitta + itnayn** = ...tamaniya...
c **sab9a – talaata** = ...waaHid tq9ol?...
d **9ashara – khamsa** = ...khamsa...

3 Lucy Abbot is on business from Newcastle in England. How would she fill in the details in this form?

ism .....Lucy Abbot.....
balad .....Ingiterra.....
jinsiyya .....ingiliziyya.....

4 Can you say these results in Arabic?

Morocco	6	France	2
Tunisia	3	Lebanon	1
Scotland	5	Syria	9
Egypt	4	Jordan	7

now you're talking!

1   **1•33** Imagine you are Olivier Jolivet, a Frenchman from Paris studying Arabic in Jordan. You get talking to a waiter in a café.

- **min wayn inta?**
- ◆ Reply, and ask him if he's from Jordan.
- **laa', ana min tuunis. wayn saakin?**
- ◆ Say you live in Paris, and ask his name.
- **ismi Jamal, marHaba.**

2   **1•34** Now take the part of a British woman, Louise Taylor, and answer the waiter's questions.

- **inti min fransa kamaan?**
- ◆ Reply.
- **wayn saakna?**
- ◆ You live in York.
- **shuu ismik?**
- ◆ Reply.

3   **1•35** Jamal would like to invite you for coffee. Listen and write his home number.

Give him your mobile number: 0971 445 376.

0196658

quiz

1 If someone tells you **ana min is-sa9uudiyya**, where are they from? *Saudi Arabia*

2 Which is the odd one out, and why? **lubnaan, maSr, maghribi** *il-maghrib /ginniya*

3 How would you tell someone that you're from England and live in London? *ana min ingiltera, saakin fi london*

4 What are the next two numbers in this sequence: **itnayn, arba9a, sitta** ...., ... *tamanya, 9ashra*

5 Would an Egyptian woman say **ana maSriyya** or **ana maSri**?

6 How would you say *He is from Syria?* *Huwwa min Suriya*

7 Would a man or a woman say **ana saakna fi Halab**? *(woman)*

8 How would you ask a business colleague for their office phone number? *shu ragm telefawn il-maktab*

Now check whether you can ...

- say what your name is *ana ismi helen*
- say where you're from *ana min must turkey mal hadith*
- say which city you live in *ana saakin fi Cambridge*
- say what your phone numbers are
- ask others for this information *shu ragm telefawn lik*
- use the numbers 0–10

It's a good idea at this stage to start organising your vocabulary learning. Write new words and phrases in a notebook or group them on index cards and review them regularly. Try sticking new words on your mirror or kitchen walls or wherever you'll see them most often. Get friends to test you on vocabulary – they don't need to be Arabic speakers.

Arabic script: 1

The varying forms of the letters are shown as:
- initial: at the beginning of a word or following a letter which only connects from the right
- medial: within a word (i.e. not at the beginning or the end)
- final: at the end of a word
- isolated: used on its own or following a letter which only connects from the right

1 Look at the following six letters. Apart from the **alif** all the others can be joined on both sides to other letters. The **alif** can only be joined from the right and may also appear as أ or إ. See page 68.

Letter	Sound	Isolated	Final	Medial	Initial
alif	aa, a, i, u	ا	ـا	ـا	ا
baa	b	ب	ـب	ـبـ	بـ
taa	t	ت	ـت	ـتـ	تـ
thaa	th	ث	ـث	ـثـ	ثـ
nuun	n	ن	ـن	ـنـ	نـ
yaa	y, ii	ي	ـي	ـيـ	يـ

The **alif** is easy to spot as it is a straight vertical line and you can see that the **yaa** is clearly recognisable because it is the only Arabic letter which has two dots below it. When an **i** appears at the end of a word it is written with the **yaa**.

2 Circle each **alif** you see in the following words:

عمان سيارة امس بريطانيا البيت انا

3 Match the following Arabic words with their written form. Do you know what any of them mean?

1 ana
2 bint
3 ab
4 ibni

5 baab
6 banaat
7 ithnayn

a اثنين
b ابني
c انا
d باب

e اب
f بنت
g بنات

Check your answers on page 90.

Arabic script: 2

1   Look at the following letters:

Letter	Sound	Isolated	Final	Medial	Initial
siin	s	س	ـس	ـسـ	سـ
shiin	sh	ش	ـش	ـشـ	شـ
kaaf	k	ك	ـك	ـكـ	كـ
laam	l	ل	ـل	ـلـ	لـ
miim	m	م	ـم	ـمـ	مـ

2   Circle the letter **miim** wherever it occurs in the following words:

أمس المغرب محطة شمس سلام مكتب

When the letter **laam** is followed by an **alif** as in the word **laa'** *no*, it takes on a special form:

Letter	Sound	Isolated	Final	Medial	Initial
laam alif	laa	لا	ـلا	لا	لا

3   The word below forms part of a well-known greeting with **laam alif** in the middle. Can you read it?

سلام

4   Match the corresponding words which all start with the letter **miim**. Do you know what any of the words mean?

1 malik   a مكتب
2 shams   b ملك
3 maktab   c شمس
4 kitaab   d كتاب

Check your answers on page 90.

haadi Farida

introducing friends and family

talking about yourself and your family

saying what you do for a living

saying how old you are

In the Arabic-speaking world, family names are used less routinely than in the West. First names are used in most social scenarios. You will also hear people being called by their title, such as **duktuur** *Doctor*. Good friends are often referred to as **akh** *brother* and **ukht** *sister*.

The words **ab** *father* and **umm** *mother* are frequently seen in proper names including place names such as **Abu Dhabi** and **Umm Qasr**. You may hear people use these words to refer to themselves e.g. **abu Ahmad** *the father of Ahmad*, **umm Hasan** *the mother of Hasan*.

If a Muslim has been on **Hajj** *pilgrimage* to the Islamic Holy sites of Mecca and Medina, after returning he or she can be referred to as **Hajj** or **Hajja** e.g. **Hajj 9umar** *pilgrim Omar*, **Hajja Maryam** *pilgrim Miriam*.

il-9aeela = family

Introducing friends and family

1 **1•36** Listen to the key language:

haada ...	This is ... (m)	**haadi ...**	This is ... (f)
... jawzi.	... my husband.	**... marti.**	... my wife.
... SaaHibi.	... my friend.	**... SaaHibti.**	... my friend.
... zamiili.	... my colleague.	**... zamiilti.**	... my colleague.

2 **1•37** Ewan Stewart has been invited to a party at Farida's flat in Beirut. She introduces him to a number of people. Can you figure out who Sinaan and Shahla are?

haada zeufti   haadi zamiilti
jawzi

bil 9arabi ...

many nouns referring to people have different masculine and feminine endings, with the feminine usually adding -a:

SaaHib _male friend_   SaaHiba _female friend_
zamiil _male colleague_   zamiila _female colleague_
To say _my_, the masculine adds -i while the feminine -a is replaced by **-ti**:

SaaHib**i** _my male friend_   SaaHib**ti** _my female friend_
zamiil**i** _my male colleague_   zamiil**ti** _my female colleague_

G1, G5

3 **1•38** Still at Farida's party, Ewan is introduced to some more people. Listen and complete the dialogue:

Yaser: **haadi ...marti... Layla.**
Ewan: **ahlan wa sahlan.**
Shahla: **ahlan fiik.**
Yaser: **wa haada ..SaHib.. Adnaan.**
Ewan: **marHaba, ya Adnaan!**
Adnaan: **marHabtayn.**
Shahla: **wa ..haadi.. SaHibti Marwa.**
Ewan: **tasharrafna.**

Who is Marwa?

4 How would you introduce the following people?
  a your wife, Suzanne   **b** your husband, John
  c your male colleague, Lutfi **d** your female friend, Jamila

haadi marti Suzanne   haada jawzi John
haada zamiili Lutfi   haada SaHibti Jamila

Talking about yourself and your family

1   **1•39** Listen to the key language:

inta mitzawwij/inti mitzawwija?	Are you married? (to m/f)
ana mitzawwij/mitzawwija.	I'm married. (m/f)
ana mish mitzawwij/mitzawwija.	I'm not married. (m/f)
9andak/9indik awlaad?	Do you have children? (to m/f)
9andi talaat banaat.	I have three daughters.
~~only~~ **9andi <u>ibn waaHid</u> wa <u>bint waaHda</u>.**	I have one son and one daughter.
maa 9andi awlaad.	I don't have (any) children.

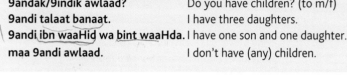

2   **1•40** Mark Jones, a student of Arabic in Syria, is chatting to two teachers, Nabiil Shukri and Hasna Sabri. Listen to their conversation, decide whether they're married and circle the correct answer.

Nabiil Shukri: (married)/not married
Hasna Sabri: (married)/not married
Mark Jones: married/(not married)

3   **1•40** Now listen again and this time write
   down how many children they have:

(handwritten: 4)

walad/awlaad
child/children or boy/boys
bint/banaat
girl/girls or daughter/daughters
ibn/abnaa' *son/sons*

	sons	daughters
Nabiil Shukri	1	3
Hasna Sabri	0	1
Mark Jones	0	0

---

bil 9arabi ...

there is no verb *to have*. Instead, endings are added onto **9and**.
These are the same endings as used to express *my, your* etc:

9andi *I have*	**9andak** *you have* (to m)	**9andu** *he has*
	9andik *you have* (to f)	**9andha** *she has*

To say *I don't have,* you use **maa** rather than **mish**: **maa 9andi**
I don't have, **maa 9andha** *she doesn't have.*   **G16**

4   **1•41** Listen to the conversation at Farida's party between Linda and
    Samia. Note down what Linda says about herself:

ana ...... *mish mitzawwij, ... maa 9andha awlaad*
maa 9andha awlaad

Saying what you do for a living

1 **1•42** Listen to the key language:

shuu shughlak/shughlik?	What's your job? (to m/f)
ana ...	I'm ...
... mudarris/mudarrisa.	... a teacher. (m/f)
... muHaasib/muHaasiba.	... an accountant. (m/f)
... mumarriD/mumarriDa.	... a nurse. (m/f)
inta Taalib?/inti Taaliba?	Are you a student? (to m/f)
laa', ana mish muhandis/muhandisa.	No, I'm not an engineer. (m/f)
ana Tabiib/Tabiiba fi mustashfa.	I'm a doctor in a hospital. (m/f)

---

bil 9arabi ...

there's no equivalent of *a*, so **Tabiib/Tabiiba** (m/f) mean both *doctor* and *a doctor* and **fi mustashfa** means *in hospital* and *in a hospital*. To say *at school* or *at university* use **fil: ana fil-jaami9a** *I'm at university*.

G9

---

2 **1•43** Listen to some of Farida's students saying what they do and match each person's name to their occupation.

1   2   3   4

a Ewan   **b** Brigitte   **c** John   **d** Hilary

3 **1•44** At the conference in Damascus, Mark Jones is briefing a visitor. Listen and note down in English what jobs people do and where.

Ahmad Khaalid ....

Leila Muraad ....

Mahmuud Saber ....

Jumaana Dalaal ....

Salah Nazmi ....

madrasa	*school*
jaami9a	*university*
maktab	*office*
sharika	*company*
ustaaz/ustaaza	*lecturer* (m/f)

4 How would you ask Mark what his job is?

Saying how old you are

1   1•45 Listen to the numbers from 11–20:

11 **Hida9sh**	16 **sitta9sh**
12 **itna9sh**	17 **sab9ata9sh**
13 **talata9sh**	18 **tamanta9sh**
14 **arba9ta9sh**	19 **tis9ata9sh**
15 **khamasta9sh**	20 **9ishriin**

2   1•46 Listen and circle the numbers you hear: 11 12 13 14 15 16 17 18 19 20

3   1•47 Listen to the key language:

9andak/9andik kam sana?	How old are you? (to m/f) *Lit.* You have how many year?
9andi khamasta9shar sana.	I'm fifteen years old. *Lit.* I have fifteen year.
shuu ismu/ismha?	What's his/her name?
kam sana 9andu/9andha?	How old is he/she?
9andu sitta9shar sana.	He is sixteen years old.
9andha sab9a siniin.	She is seven years old.

---

bil 9arabi ...

when using numbers with nouns, 3–10 use the noun in the plural, and drop their final **-a.** Anything over 10 uses the noun in the singular, and numbers 11–19 add **-ar**:
talaat mudarrisiin *three teachers* (m), **itna9shar mudarris** *twelve teachers* (m).
You may have noticed certain nouns change quite dramatically from singular to plural. These have to be learned as you come across them.   **G2, G20**

---

4   1•48 Nabiil Shukri has invited Mark Jones to his house in Damascus and introduces him to his son Muhammed and his friends Hasan and George. Listen and write how old they are.
    Muhammed ....   Hasan ....   George ....

5   1•49 At Farida's party one of the students asks Shahla about her children. Who is older, Latifa or Sinaan?

put it all together

1 Which answer fits best the question?

a	inta mitzawwij, ya Munir? 3	1	laa', ana mudarrisa.
b	ibnak 9andu kam sana? 4	2	9andha khams siniin.
c	9andik awlaad, ya Mervat? 6	3	laa', ana mish mitzawwij.
d	shuu shughlak, ya John? 5	4	9andu sitta9shar sana.
e	inti Taaliba? 1	5	ana muHaasib.
f	bintik 9andha kam sana? 2	6	aywa, 9andi talaat awlaad.

2 This is Ahmad's family tree:

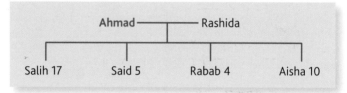

Ahmad ——— Rashida

Salih 17   Said 5   Rabab 4   Aisha 10

Choose the correct option.

a Ahmad   • mitzawwij   • mitzawwija
b Ahmad 9andu   • arba9a banaat   • arba9a awlaad
c Rabab 9andha   • arba9a siniin   • arba9ta9shar sana
d Aisha 9andha   • 9ashar siniin   • khams siniin
e Salih 9andu   • sitta9shar sana   • sab9ata9shar sana

3 How would Munir introduce these people?

Saida: wife, teacher
Ashraf: friend, married, accountant
Lina: colleague, not married, doctor

Haadi marti, hiyya mudarrisa
Haada SaHibi, huwa mitzawwij wa huwa muHaasib
Haadi zamiilti, hiyya mish mitzawwija wa hiyya Tabiba.

now you're talking!

1   **1•50** Answer the following questions as if you were David
    Warren, a teacher from Manchester, married to Rachel, with
    a daughter Alison, who's 12.

    - **ahlan. min wayn inta?**
    - **shuu ismak?**
    - **haadi martak?**
    - **shuu shuglak?**
    - **wa 9andak awlaad?**
    - **kam sana 9andha?**

2   **1•51** While on a train you get talking to the man sitting next
    to you who shows you some photos.

    - Ask if he's married.
    - ◆ **aywa, ana mitzawwij.**
    - Point to a picture and ask if that's his wife.
    - ◆ **aywa, ismha Hiba.**
    - Ask if he has children
    - ◆ **9andi ibn waaHid.**
    - Ask his name.
    - ◆ **ismu Hussein.**
    - Ask how old Hussein is.
    - ◆ **9andu tis9ata9shar sana.**
    - Ask if Hussein is at school.
    - ◆ **laa', huwwa Taalib fi jaami9at dimashq.**

quiz

1 What is a **mustashfa**? *hospitl*
2 How do you say *one daughter and one son*? *ibn Waahid* *bint Waahi?*
3 What is **9ishriin** minus **arba9ta9shar**? *sitta 6*
4 If someone is twenty years old would they use **siniin** or **sana** to give their age?
5 Is **Taaliba** a male or female student?
6 How would you introduce your friend, Rana? *Haadi Sahbti Rana*
7 If someone says **shuu ismha?** are they talking about a man or a woman?
8 How would a woman say *I'm not married*? *ana mish mitzawijja*
9 **maa 9andi awlaad** means *I don't have children*. So how would you say *I don't have a mobile*? *maa 9andi mobayl*

Now check whether you can ...

- introduce friends and colleagues
- say whether you're married or not
- say if you have children
- talk about your occupation
- ask others for the above information
- use the numbers 11-20
- give your age
- ask how old other people are

A good way to practise talking about your family is to find a **Suura** *photograph* with lots of your family members in it, such as a wedding group. Point to each person and say their name, who they are in relation to you, how old they are. You might be able to say what some of them do for a living, and if there are different nationalities involved you could mention that too.

Arabic script: 3

1   Look at the following new letters, all of which can only be joined from the right.

Letter	Sound	Isolated	Final	Medial	Initial
daal	d	د	ـد	ـد	د
dhaal	dh	ذ	ـذ	ـذ	ذ
raa	r	ر	ـر	ـر	ر
zaa	z	ز	ـز	ـز	ز
waw	w, uu	و	ـو	ـو	و

2   Circle the letter **raa** in the following words. Do you recognise any of them?

عربي   رقم   يسار   سيارة   سيارة   مدرسة

3   Match the following words:

1 zaar	2 naar	a دور	b نور
3 daar	4 baar	c سور	d ذاب
5 dhaab	6 nuur	e دار	f زار
7 duur	8 suur	g بار	h نار

4   Match the following Arabic first names with the Arabic script:

1 **Zaynab**   a مراد
2 **Anwar**   b زيد
3 **Zayd**   c رمزي
4 **Ramzi**   d زينب
5 **Mourad**   e أنور

5   Can you identify these two Arab countries?

1 السودان   2 سوريا

Check your answers on page 90.

Arabic script: 4

1 Look at the following letters:

Letter	Sound	Isolated	Final	Medial	Initial
jiim	j	ج	ج	ﺠ	ﺟ
Haa	H	ح	ح	ﺤ	ﺣ
khaa	kh	خ	خ	ﺨ	ﺧ
haa	h	ه	ﺪ	ﻬ	ﻫ

2 Put a circle around the letter **haa** each time you see it in the following words:

إسمه   هذا   مهندس   سهل   هذه   هناك

3 Match these signs that you're likely to see at an airport:

1 **jamaarik** *customs*   a جوازات

2 **jawaazaat** *passports*   b دخول

3 **dukhuul** *entrance*   c خروج

4 **khuruuj** *exit*   d جمارك

Many nouns ending in -a, for example **madrasa** مدرسة *school*, end with the **ta marbuuTa**. This looks like a **haa** with two dots above it: ة or ﺔ. The **ta marbuuTa** is also used on the end of adjectives to make them feminine: **kibiira** كبيرة *big*, **Saghiira** صغيرة *small*.

4 Read the information about the facilities available at the Safir hotel in Beirut and tick what's available from the list on the right:

1 إنترنيت   a **Hammaam sibaaHa** *swimming pool*

2 حمام سباحة   b **maT9am lubnaani** *Lebanese restaurant*

3 بنك   c **maktab safar** *travel agency*

d **bank**

e **internet**

Check your answers on page 90.

waaHid 'ahwa, min faDlak

ordering tea and coffee

... and other drinks

offering, accepting, refusing

asking and paying for the bill

Coffee and tea are popular drinks in the Arab World and the café is the traditional meeting place. *Arabic tea* **shaay 9arabi** is often served black *with mint* **bi na9na9** and in a small glass. Coffee in most Arab countries is similar to Turkish coffee and is quite strong, served either **maZbuuT** *semi-sweet* or **sukkar ziyaada** *with extra sugar*. In some of the countries of the Levant, the coffee is spiced **bi Habb il-haal** *with cardamom* and served with **kaas mayya** *a glass of water*.

In hotels and larger cafés, you can also have English tea served with milk and a wide range of Western-style coffees.

When you're invited to an Arab home, you will traditionally be served with either tea or coffee depending on the local custom.

Ordering tea and coffee

1 **1.52** Listen to the key language:

shuu b-tHibb/b-tHibbi?	What would you like? (to m/f)
biddi ...	I'd like ...
... waaHid shaay	... one tea
... wa itnayn 'ahwa.	... and two coffees.
maZbuuT	semi-sweet
bi/biduun sukkar	with/without sugar
bi Haliib aw biduun Haliib?	With milk or without milk?
min faDlak/min faDlik	please (to m/f)
HaaDir.	OK.

bil 9arabi ...

when ordering food and drinks, the normal rules of using numbers with nouns are suspended. The convention is to use the countable number with the singular noun, e.g: **itnayn shaay** *two teas*, **talaata shaay** *three teas* etc.

G20

2 **1.53** Farida invites some of her students out to a café on the Corniche in Beirut. Listen and make a note of what she orders:

a Number of teas with milk ......1......................

b Number of teas without milk ......2...............

c Number of coffees (semi-sweet) ....3..............

d Number of coffees without sugar ....1............

3 **1.54** Amal is ordering coffee and tea for herself and her friend Ruba at the Café al-Andalous. Listen and fill the gaps in the dialogue:

● .shuu. **b-tHibbi?**

◆ **min faDlak, biddi waaHid** .ahwa. **wa waaHid** .shaay..

● ....bi... **sukkar aw** .biduun. **sukkar?**

◆ **shaay biduun sukkar, wa 'ahwa** .maZbut.

● **HaaDir.**

... and other drinks

1 **1.55** Listen to the key language:

ayy khidma?	Can I help you? *Lit.* which service
ayy 9aSiir 9andak/9andik?	Which juices do you have? (to m/f)
fiih ...	There is ...
... 9aSiir burtu'aan.	... orange juice.
... 9aSiir lamuun.	... lemon juice.
biddi itnayn 9aSiir manga.	I'd like two mango juices.
9andak/9andik biira?	Do you have beer? (to m/f)
laa', maa fiih biira.	No, there isn't any beer.

2 **1.56** Ewan Stewart is ordering some drinks in a café in Baalbek. Listen and tick from the list below the drinks he orders. What else does Ewan ask the waiter?

9aSiir shammaam *melon juice*	**9aSiir manga**
9aSiir tuffaaH *apple juice*	**9ilbat cola** *can of cola*
'aniinat mayya ma9daniyya	**9aSiir burtu'aan**
a bottle of mineral water	**biira**

3 **1.57** Maha and Samira stop for refreshments. Listen to Maha speaking to the waiter. What does she order? Why doesn't she order apple juice?

---

bil 9arabi ...

the word for *to want* varies from region to region. **biddi** *I want/would like* is used widely throughout the Levant. It is not a verb and uses the possessive endings (*my/your* etc.):

biddi *I want*   **biddak** *you want* (to m)   **biddik** *you want* (to f)

G16

---

4 How would you order the following from a waitress?

1 tea with milk
2 semi-sweet coffees
1 apple juice
2 melon juices
1 bottle of mineral water
3 beers

Offering, accepting and refusing

1 **1.58** Listen to the key language:

shuu b-tishrab/b-tishrabi? What would you like to drink? (to m/f) *Lit.* What you drink?

b-tHibb/b-tHibbi shaay aw 'ahwa? Would you like tea or coffee? (to m/f)

b-aakhud cola bass. I'll just have a cola. *Lit.* I take cola only.

9ashaanak/9ashaanik? For you? (to m/f)

9ashaani ... For me ...

laa', shukran. No, thanks.

Tayyib. Fine. OK.

---

bil 9arabi ...

verbs have both prefixes and endings in the present tense:

	like	*take*	*drink*
I	aHibb	aakhud	ashrab
you (m)	tiHibb	taakhud	tishrab
you (f)	tiHibbi	taakhdi	tishrabi

In the Levant a **b-** prefix is also added before the verb in the present tense. To say you don't do something, you put **maa** first:
maa b-aHibb *I don't like*, **maa b-tishrabi** *you* (f) *don't drink*. **G10**

---

2 **1.59** Nabiil Sha'aban is at a café in Damascus with two friends, Nadia and Hasan. Listen and note what drinks they decide to have.

Nadia .... Hasan ....

3 **1.60** Hasan invites Nabiil for coffee the next day. Number their conversation below in the right order and then listen to check.

biddak 'aniinat mayya kamaan?	5
9ashaani... b-aakhud 'ahwa bass.	7
ahlan, ya Nabiil! kiif il-haal?	1
ana b-aakhud 'ahwa bi Haliib, min faDlak.	4
laa' shukran, maa biddi mayya, w-inta?	6
bi-khayr shukran. w-inta?	2
il-Hamdullilaah. shuu b-tishrab?	3

Asking and paying for the bill

1 **1.61** Listen to the following numbers:

20	9ishriin	21	waaHid wa 9ishriin
30	talatiin	22	itnayn wa 9ishriin
40	arba9iin	23	talaata wa 9ishriin
50	khamsiin	24	arba9a wa 9ishriin
60	sittiin	25	khamsa wa 9ishriin
70	saba9iin	26	sitta wa 9ishriin
80	tamaniin	27	sab9a wa 9ishriin
90	tis9iin	28	tamanya wa 9ishriin
100	miyya	29	tis9a wa 9ishriin

2 **1.62** You're going to hear all but one of the following numbers. Which one is it?

30   65   40   33   20   78   50   22   44

3 **1.63** Say the following numbers out loud, then listen to them to see how you did.

26   53   61   74   77   81   99   100

4 **1.64** Listen to the key language:

il-Hisaab, min faDlak/min faDlik.	The bill, please. (to m/f)
khalli il-baa'i 9ashaanak/9ashaanik.	Keep the change. (to m/f)
shukran kitiir.	Thank you very much.
9afwan.	You're welcome.
itfaDDal/itfaDDali.	Here you are. (to m/f)

5 **1.65** Listen to the waiter telling Hasan Shukri how much his order is and fill in the answers below. Listen out for **il-majmuu9** *the total*.

coffee ……… juice ……… total ………

6 **1.66** Amal is paying the bill at the Café al-Andalous. Can you figure out how much tip she leaves for the waiter?

put it all together

1 Choose a suitable response from the box below

   a   **shuu b-tHibb?** *5*

   b   **il-Hisaab, min faDlak.** *1*

   c   **ayy 9aSiir 9indik?** *2 (or 4)*

   d   **fiih biira?** *4*

   e   **khalli il-baa'i 9ashaanak.** *3*

> **1 itfaDDal.**
>
> **2 fiih 9aSiir manga wa 9aSiir shammaam.**
>
> **3 shukran.**
>
> **4 laa', maa fiih.**
>
> **5 biddi 'aniinat mayya, min faDlak.**

2 Say these numbers in Arabic then write the answers.

   1 26 + 67   **2** 45 + 33   **3** 38 + 51

   4 74 − 42   **5** 81 − 28   **6** 90 − 66

1 - talaata wa tis9iin
2 - tamanya u sab9iin
3 - tis9a wa tamaniin
4 - ithnayn wa talatiin
5 - itnayn wa khamsiin
6 - Arba'a wa 'ishriin

3 What has been ordered to drink?

   a   **b-aakhud waaHid shaay bi sukkar.**

   b   **biddi talaata 9aSiir burtu'aan.**

   c   **biddi itnayn 'ahwa maZbuuT.**

   d   **b-ashrab 9aSiir lamuun.**

   e   **9ashaani 'ahwa wa 'aniinat mayya ma9daniyya.**

now you're talking!

1   **1.67** You're in a café in Damascus with some friends who don't speak Arabic.

- **ayy khidma?**
- ◆ Order two semi-sweet coffees and one tea.
- **bi Haliib aw biduun Haliib?**
- ◆ Say with milk.
- **HaaDir.**

2   **1.68** You're ready to leave the café.

- Ask the waiter for the bill.
- ◆ **itfaDDali, saba9iin lira.**
- Offer him 80 Syrian pounds, and tell him to keep the change.
- ◆ **shukran kitiir. ma9a as-salaama.**
- ◆ Say goodbye.

3   **1.69** You're at a party in Beirut.

- **ahlan. shuu b-tishrabi?**
- ◆ Say hello to him, and ask if there's any beer.
- **laa', maa fiih biira. 9andi 9aSiir burtu'aan aw 9aSiir tuffaaH.**
- ◆ Say you'll have an orange juice, please.
- **itfaDDali.**

quiz

1 If you say **shukran kitiir**, what will you often hear in reply? *[handwritten]*
2 How do you say *only*? *bas* *[handwritten]*
3 What is **tamanya wa tamaniin**? *88* *[handwritten]*
4 Given that **rumaan** is *pomegranate*, how would you ask a waitress *Do you have pomegranate juice*? *9andak 9aasir rumaan? [handwritten]*
5 When ordering a drink from a man, how do you say *please*? *min faDlak [handwritten]*
6 Would you use **9ashaani**, **9ashaanak** or **9ashaanik** to order for yourself?
7 How do you ask for something *without sugar*? *bidun sukkar [handwritten]*
8 What is **il-Hisaab**? *bill [handwritten]*

Now check whether you can ...

- order tea and different types of coffee
- order cold drinks
- ask someone what they would like to drink
- accept or decline when you're offered a drink
- use the numbers 20–100
- ask for the bill

Teaching another person the Arabic words for various items could help you to remember them better yourself. Enlist the co-operation of a willing friend or member of the family, and when you're out with them, in a pub or a café, teach them how you would place your order for drinks and/or snacks in Arabic.

> SabaaH il-khayr

> 9andak kam sana?

> haadi marti

> ana mish mitzawwij(a)

> ahlan wa sahlan

> wayn saakna?

> ana bi-khayr, shukran

> tasharrafna

1 Which of the above expressions would you use to …

a say hello   *ahlan wa sahlan*
b say you're well, thanks   *ana bi-khayr, shukran*
c say pleased to meet you   *tasharrafna*
d ask how old someone is   *9andak kam sana?*
e say good morning   *SabaaH il-khayr*
f introduce your wife   *haadi marti*
g ask a woman where she lives   *wayn saakna?*
h say that you're not married   *ana mish mitzawwij(a)*

2 Identify the odd one out:

a	shaay	SabaaH	biira	mayya	'ahwa
b	mudarris	muhandis	mumarriD	mubayl	muHaasib
c	madrasa	mustashfa	maktab	jaami9a	mitzawwij
d	urduni	maSri	sa9uudi	maghribi	tuunisiyya
e	akh	ukht	ab	ibn	jawz
f	burtu'aan	tuffaaH	manga	9ilba	lamuun
g	bint	zamiila	SaaHiba	sharika	mudarrisa
h	ahlan	marHaba	masaa il-khayr	is-salaam 9alaykum	Tayyib

3 Look at the information required for the following form. What are the questions you'd need to ask a man to complete it?

Name:	*shuu ismak?*
Age:	*9andak kam sanaa?*
Nationality:	*Min wayn inta? shuu jinsiyat...*
City of residence:	*Wayn saakin? wayn jaa...?*
Occupation:	*shu shaylak / shughl?*
Marital status:	*inti mitzawij / mitzawija*
Children:	*9andak awlaad?*

a ....

b ....

c ....

d ....

e ....

f ....

g ....

4 **1•70** Listen to some delegates at a conference in Jordan introducing themselves. Choose the right nationality from the list and complete the table:

> lubnaani lubnaaniyya suuri suuriyya
> ingliizi ingliiziyya sa9uudi sa9uudiyya
> maghribi maghribiyya maSri maSriyya

il-ism *name*	il-jinsiyya *nationality*	makaan il-iqaama *place of residence*
Ahmad	*miSri*	**il-qaahira**
Lutfi	*suuri*	**dimashq**
Naima	*maghribiyya*	**ir-ribaaT**
Suhail	*sa9uudi*	**ir-riyaaD**
Nadia	*lubnaaniyya*	**bayruut**
Susan	*ingliiziyya*	**Leeds**

5 **1•71** Listen to the international dialling codes for these countries and add the missing numbers.

1	liibya	00 _218_	2	il-maghrib	00 _212_
3	maSr	00 _20_	4	il-imaaraat	00 _971_
5	lubnaan	00 _961_	6	suuriya	00 _963_
7	il-urdun	00 _962_	8	is-sa9uudiyya	00 _966_

6 What questions would you need to ask in order to receive the following answers?

a _ayy 9asiir 9ads?_ ? fiih 9aSiir manga, wa 9aSiir tuffaaH wa 9aSiir shammaam.

b _shu bTHbb?_ ? biddi itnayn shaay, min faDlik.

c _bi aw bidun Haliib?_ ? biduun Haliib.

d _9indak 9asiir lamuun?_ ? laa', maa fiih 9aSiir lamuun.

e _9ashaani?_ ? 9ashaani ... b-aakhud 'ahwa bass.

7 **1•72** Practise saying the names of some of the major cities in the Arab world. Listen to check and then match them to their English translations.

> 1 Halab _d_   2 bayruut _i_   3 il-qaahira _g_   4 ir-riyaaD _j_
> 5 9ammaan _h_   6 jadda _a_   7 tuunis _e_
> 8 dimashq _c_   9 iskandariyya _f_   10 ir-ribaaT _b_

> a Jeddah   b Rabat   c Damascus   d Aleppo
> e Tunis   f Alexandria   g Cairo
> h Amman   i Beirut   j Riyadh

8 **1•73** While waiting at the Abdalleh bus station in Amman you overhear two people talking. Listen then complete their profiles by ticking the correct boxes:

Mona works as a	☐ nurse	☒ doctor
Mona lives in	☐ Rabat	☒ London
Lutfi is	☒ Jordanian	☐ Saudi
Lutfi is	☒ married	☐ single
Mona has a	☐ husband	☒ partner/boyfriend
Lutfi has	☐ no children	☒ one son

9 Look at the drinks menu from Café Salaam and write down in Arabic how much the following items cost.

Café Salaam

shaay	khamsa wa arba3iin	45 L.S.
'ahwa	sab3a wa sittiin	67 L.S.
9aSiir lamuun	tis3a wa sab3iin	79 L.S.
mayya ma9daniyya	tamanya wa tamaniin	88 L.S.
shaay bi na9na9	khamsa wa khamsiin	55 L.S.
'ahwa bi Haliib	talaata wa sab3iin	73 L.S.
9aSiir manga	arba3a wa tis3iin	94 L.S.
9aSiir tuffaaH	sitta wa tamaniin	86 L.S.

a mint tea .... **b** lemon juice ....

c mango juice .... **d** apple juice ....

10 Practise ordering some drinks using the phrases learnt in Unit 4. Remember that you can use **biddi** *I'd like,* **b-aakhud** *I'll have,* **9ashaani** *for me.*

a two **b** one **c** three **d** four

e one **f** two **g** five **h** one

law samaHt, fiih maT9am hawn?

asking what there is

... and whereabouts it is

finding out which day places are open

... and what time they're open

Opening times in the Arab World do vary from country to country but as a rule Friday is the weekly day off. In many countries Saturday is also a day off. This will apply to banks and post offices, although foreign exchange facilities are usually open in large hotels every day. North African countries such as Tunisia and Morocco have Sunday as their main day off.

Opening hours are generally 8am-2pm. Some offices open again in the evening. Shops in big cities such as Damascus and Cairo will stay open until 8pm and often later.

There are few **makaatib isti9laamaat** *tourist information offices*. You can ask for local information at hotel receptions, or even hire a taxi for the day with a driver-guide. This is quite common and is good value.

Asking what there is

1 **1•74** Listen to the key language:

mumkin ti'uul/ti'uuli li …	Can you tell me … (to m/f)
fiih Saydaliyya hawn?	Is there a chemist's here?
fiih maT9am hawn?	Is there a restaurant here?
laa', maa fiih Saydaliyya hawn.	No, there isn't a chemist's here.
aywa, fiih maTaa9im kitiir.	Yes, there are many restaurants.

2 **1•75** Look at this list of places. Listen and practise saying them:

suu' market	**maktab bariid** post office	**dukkaan** shop	**dakaakiin** shops
bank bank	**ba'aal** grocer's	**maqha internet** internet café	**matHaf** museum
suubermarket supermarket	**fundu'** hotel	**maHaTTa** station	**jaami9** mosque

3 **1•76** Hiba Mustafa, the receptionist at the Ommayad Hotel in Damascus, tells a group of guests about the district around the hotel. Make a note of the four places she mentions.

1 ....maktab bariid........ 2 ....suu'........ 3 ....bank........ 4 ....dakaakiin........

---

bil 9arabi …

all nouns in Arabic – not just those referring to people – are either masculine or feminine, e.g. **maT9am** *restaurant* is masculine whereas **Saydaliyya** *chemist's* is feminine.

Most feminine nouns end in -a, e.g. **maHaTTa** *station*, although there are some exceptions such as **umm** *mother* and **shams** *sun*. Most nouns not ending in -a are masculine e.g. **bayt** *house*. **G1**

---

4 **1•77** Now listen as people ask Hiba questions, and tick or cross the availability of the following.

internet café ✓   supermarket ✓   grocer's ✗   museum ✓

ba'il

... and whereabouts it is

1 **1•78** Listen to the key language:

wayn il-bank biZ-ZabT?	Where is the bank exactly?
il-bank mi'aabil il-fundu'.	The bank is <u>opposite</u> the hotel.
iS-Saydaliyya <u>janb</u> il-mustashfa.	The chemist's is <u>next to</u> the hospital.
maktab il-bariid <u>waraa</u> il-madrasa.	The post office is <u>behind</u> the school.
il-maHaTTa fi <u>wasT</u> il-madiina.	The station is in <u>the centre</u> of town.
is-suu' <u>ba9d</u> maHaTTat il-qiTaar.	The market is <u>past</u> the railway station.

---

bil 9arabi ...

as you saw on page 21, when two nouns are used together you only use **il-** *the* on the second noun: **maktab il-bariid** *the post office* Lit. *office the post,* **wasT il-madiina** *the centre of town* Lit. *centre the town.*

If the first noun normally ends in -a then this becomes -at: **madrasa** *school,* **madras<u>at</u> il-awlaad** *the boys' school;* **maHaTTa** *station,* **maHaTT<u>at</u> il-qiTaar** *the railway station.* **G6**

---

2 **1•79** Shahla is staying at a hotel in Alexandria and asks the receptionist to point out various places on her map. Listen and work out what A, B, C and D are.

3 **1•80** Shahla asks a passer-by where the museum is. Where is it in relation to the station and the mosque?

4 **1•80** Listen again and note down how she asks where the museum is. ....

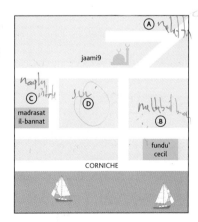

5 law samaHt, fiih maT9am hawn? **51**

Finding out which day places are open

1   1•81 Listen to the key language:

il-bank maftuuH aymta?	When is the bank open?
maktab il-bariid maftuuH il-yawm?	Is the post office open today?
huwwa maftuuH/hiyya maftuuHa ...	It is open ... (m/f)
... kull yawm.	... every day.
... min yawm il-aHad li yawm il-khamiis.	... from Sunday to Thursday.
huwwa ma'fuul/hiyya ma'fuula ...	It is closed ... (m/f)

---

bil 9arabi ...

maftuuH/maftuuHa *open* (m/f) and ma'fuul/ma'fuula *closed* (m/f) must agree in gender with what they describe:

il-maT9am maftuuH *the restaurant is open*

iS-Saydaliyya maftuuHa *the chemist's is open*   G13

---

2   1•82 Listen to the days of the week and practise saying them.

3   1•83 Back at the hotel Shahla asks at reception when places are open. Tick the right box.

yawm il-aHad	Sunday
yawm il-itnayn	Monday
yawm it-talaata	Tuesday
yawm il-arba9a	Wednesday
yawm il-khamiis	Thursday
yawm il-jum9a	Friday
yawm is-sabt	Saturday

	every day	Mon–Sat	Sun–Thurs
is-suubermarket	✓		
iS-Saydaliyya		✓	
maktab il-bariid			✓

4   1.83 Listen to the conversation again. Is the post office open today? What does the receptionist say?

5   1.84 Mark Jones is at the reception of the Baron Hotel. Listen to the dialogue and fill in the gaps. You'll hear **bass** *but* and **Hadii'a** *park*.

- law samaHt, il-matHaf maftuuH .... yawm?
- il-matHaf .... il-yawm, bass huwwa .... bukra.
- il-Hadii'a .... kull yawm.

... and what time they're open

1 **1•85** Listen to the key language:

ayy saa9a ...	What time ...
... b-yiftaH/b-tiftaH?	... does it open? (m/f)
... b-yi'fil/b-ti'fil?	... does it close? (m/f)
ayy saa9a b-yiftaH il-matHaf?	What time does the museum open?
b-yiftaH is-saa9a tis9a.	It opens at 9 o'clock. (m)
ayy saa9a b-yi'fil is-suubermarket?	What time does the supermarket close?
b-yi'fil is-saa9a arba9a.	It closes at 4 o'clock. (f)
huwwa maftuuH min is-saa9a tis9a lis-saa9a talaata.	It is open from 9 o'clock to 3 o'clock. (m)

2 **1•86** Practise saying the times below using **is-saa9a** *the time is*.

a b c d e

---

bil 9arabi ...

verbs agree with, i.e. match, their noun in terms of gender, masculine or feminine:

il-bank b-yiftaH *the bank opens* (m)
il-madrasa b-tiftaH *the school opens* (f)

G10

---

3 **1•87** Listen and note the opening and closing times of these places

		opens	closes
a	museum	9	4
b	restaurant	6	10
c	station	5	9

4 How would you ask what time the market opens?

ayy saa9a (is-suu') b-yiftiH?

put it all together

1   Match the phrases.

a	**is-suu' maftuuH kull yawm.** 7	(1) There isn't an internet café here.
b	**ayy saa9a b-yi'fil il-matHaf?** 5	(2) Can you tell me? (to m)
c	**il-maHaTTa mi'aabil il-mustashfa.** 6	(3) Where is the post office?
d	**il-maktab ma'fuul yawm il-jum9a.** 8	(4) The bank opens at nine o'clock.
e	**wayn maktab il-bariid?**	(5) What time does the museum close?
f	**mumkin ti'uul li?** 2	(6) The station is opposite the hospital.
g	**maa fiih maqha internet hawn.** (1)	(7) The market is open every day.
h	**il-bank b-yiftaH is-saa9a tis9a.** (4)	(8) The office is closed on Fridays.

2   Read the information below, and practise telling an Arabic-speaking visitor about the opening and closing times shown as in the following example:

bank: Mon–Fri, 9:00–4:00.
il-bank maftuuH min yawm il-itnayn li yawm il-jum9a. b-yiftaH is-saa9a tis9a. b-yi'fil is-saa9a arba9a.

   a   museum: Tues–Thurs, 9:00–5:00.

   b   chemist's: every day, 8:00–7:00.

   c   grocer's: Mon–Sat, 10:00–6:00.

3   Describe what there is in your town. Starting with **fi madiinti** *in my town.* Remember to use **fiih ...** *there is/there are ...*, and **kitiir** *many.*

1   1•88 You're visiting Aleppo and you ask a man at a kiosk for some information.

- Say *excuse me* and ask if there's an internet café in the area.
- **aywa, fiih maqha internet mi'aabil il-bank.**
- Now ask where the **9alaa' id-diin** *Aladdin* restaurant is.
- **il-maT9am janb is-suu'.**
- Thank him and say goodbye.
- **allaah yisalmak.**

2   1•89 Back at the Baron Hotel in Aleppo you ask Rachida the receptionist about opening times.

- Say *excuse me* and ask what time the post office opens.
- **maktab il-bariid b-yiftaH is-saa9a tamanya.**
- Now ask if it's open every day.
- **laa', huwwa ma'fuul yawm il-aHad.**
- Ask if the museum is open today.
- **laa', huwwa ma'fuul il-yawm. il-matHaf maftuuH bukra.**
- Thank her.
- **ahlan wa sahlan.**

quiz

1 What comes next: **yawm il-arba9a, yawm il-khamiis ...** ?
2 How do you say *when* and *where* in Arabic?
3 What are the opposites of these words: **fiih, ma'fuul, b-yiftaH**?
4 What is the plural of **dukkaan**?
5 If someone says **il-bank mi'aabil il-maHaTTa**, is it *next to* or *opposite* the station?
6 Which is the odd one out: **Saydaliyya, fundu', waraa**? What does it mean?
7 Which would you expect to be open **kull yawm: il-matHaf** or **il-mustashfa**?
8 Given **maHaTTat il-qiTaar** means *the railway station* lit. *station of the railway*, how would you say *the hotel restaurant*?

Now check whether you can ...

- approach someone politely
- understand and say the words for places in a town
- ask if there's a particular place nearby
- understand basic phrases as to where a place is
- ask when a place is open
- recognise days of the week
- understand basic times

To help you remember the Arabic you learn, bring it into your everyday life as much as you can. Practise saying what there is and isn't in your home town. You could also imagine you're telling an Arabic-speaking visitor when places are open where you live, for example, banks, supermarkets and shops.

Arabic script: 5

1 Look at the following four letters:

Letter	Sound	Isolated	Final	Medial	Initial
Saad	S	ص	ص	صـ	صـ
Daad	D	ض	ض	ضـ	ضـ
Taa	T	ط	ط	ط	ط
DHaa	DH	ظ	ظ	ظـ	ظـ

2 Circle the letter **Taa** each time you see it in the following words. Do you recognise any of them?

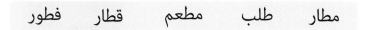

فطور   قطار   مطعم   طلب   مطار

3 If you see this sign on a motorway approaching **il-maTaar id-dawli** *the international airport*, which one of the United Arab Emirates are you in?

مطار أبو ظبي الدولي ✈

4 You are at Marrakesh station looking at the **il-wuSuul** الوصول *arrivals* and **idh-dhahaab** الذهاب *departures* board.

il-wuSuul	الوصول	idh-dhahaab	الذهاب
09.30	طنجة	09.20	الجديدة
10.00	الرباط	09.35	الدار البيضاء
11.05	المطار	10.40	طنجة

1 What time does the train for Tangiers (**Tanja**) leave?
2 Has the 10.00 train arrived from Rabat (**ir-ribaaT**) or Al Jadida (**il-jadiida**)?
3 Is the Casablanca (**id-daar il-bayDa**) train departing or arriving?
4 Is there a train to the airport between 09.30 and 11.00?

Check your answers on page 90.

Arabic script: 6

1 Look at the following two letters:

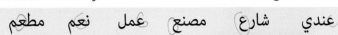

Letter	Sound	Isolated	Final	Medial	Initial
9ayn	9	ع	ع	ـعـ	ع
ghayn	gh	غ	غ	ـغـ	غ

2 Circle the letter **9ayn** wherever it occurs in the following words:

مطعم   نعم   عمل   مصنع   شارع   عندي

3 You want to order a mint tea (**shaay bi na9na9**) and a grape juice (**9aSiir 9inab**). Can you find them on the menu opposite?

a   ماء معدنية
b   عصير تفاح
c   عصير عنب
d   شاي بنعنع

alif maqSuura appears at the end of certain words and is pronounced **a**. It looks like a **yaa** without the two dots (ى or ى) as in: **mustashfa** مستشفى *hospital*.

alif tanwiin is an **alif** with two small lines above it اً and is pronounced **an** as in **shukran** شكراً *thank you*.

4 Match the following Arabic words ending with **alif maqSuura**:

1 mabna *building*   **2 maqha** *cafe*   **3 9ala** *on*   **4 ila** *towards*

a مقهى   b إلى   c مبنى   d على

5 Your hotel in Beirut is on **shaari9 al-maghrib** *Morocco Street*. Tick the correct street name from the list of streets below:

1 شارع لبنان   2 شارع عبد العزيز

3 شارع المغرب   4 شارع الحمراء

Check your answers on page 90.

kiif aruuH lis-suu'?

asking the way

... and following directions

making enquiries

... and getting help to understand

The majority of Arab towns and cities have mediaeval Islamic 'cores' with very narrow streets and alleyways often surrounded by ancient walls. Some of the largest of these cities are **marraaksh** *Marrakesh* and **faas** *Fez* in Morocco, **dimashq** *Damascus* and **Halab** *Aleppo* in Syria, and **il-qaahira** *Cairo* in Egypt. Attached to the old cities where the famous **aswaa'** *souks/ markets* are located are the more modern sections which were developed during the Ottoman, French or British colonial periods. Cities in countries under French rule often have areas modelled on the Parisian-style layout.

The Arab world also has great port cities such as **id-daar il-bayDa** *Casablanca*, **il-jazaa'ir** *Algiers*, **iskandariyya** *Alexandria*, **bayruut** *Beirut* and **jadda** *Jeddah*.

Asking the way

على (ala)
- on -

1   **2•1** Listen to the key language:

wayn a'rab suubermarket?	Where is the nearest supermarket?
kiif aruuH lis-suu'?	How do I get to the market? *Lit.* How do I go to the market?
huwwa/hiyya ...	It's ... (m/f)
... 9ala Tuul.	... straight ahead.
... fi aakhir ish-shaari9.	... at the end of the road.
... fi awwal shaari9 9al-yasaar.	... on the first street on the left.
... fi taani shaari9 9al-yamiin.	... on the second street on the right.
aasif/asfa. maa b-a9raf.	I'm sorry. I don't know. (m/f)

2   **2•2** Whilst on a visit to Amman, Sarah Walker asks where the market is. Listen and pick out from the above list the two pieces of information she's given.

a ....*huwwa 9ala tuul*.................... b ....*fi aakhir ih-thaari9*...............

---

bil 9arabi ...

ordinal numbers i.e. *first, second* etc., which are adjectives, can come before or after the noun. When they come before the noun they use the masculine form: **awwal shaari9** *(the) first street*, **taani shaari9** *(the) second street*.

When they come after the noun they have to agree with the noun in gender, and both the ordinal number and the noun take **il-** *the*: **ish-shaari9 it-taani** *the second street* Lit. *the street the second*, **taani madrasa** *second school*, **il-madrasa it-taanya** *the second school* Lit. *the school the second*.   **G7**

---

3   **2•3** Listen as Mark Jones asks for directions, then answer the questions below.
   supermarket
   • Where does Mark want to go?   • What does the first person say?
   • What directions is he given?   *maa b-a3raf.*
   fi taani shaari9 9al-yasaar

4   **2•4** How would you ask a female passer-by how you get to the bank? Now listen as she gives you some information and note its exact location.   *la*

... and following directions

1 **2•5** Listen to the key language:

ruuH/ruuHi li ishaarat il-muruur.	Go as far as the traffic lights. (to m/f)
ruuH/ruuHi 9ala Tuul.	Go straight on. (to m/f)
liff/liffi yamiin. / yawar (left)	Turn right. (to m/f)
khud/khudi ...	Take ... (to m/f)
... awwal yasaar.	... the first left.
... taani yamiin.	... the second right.

2 **2•6** Sarah is being given directions to the bank, museum and market. Listen and label the boxes marked 1 to 3 on the map. You'll hear **ba9dayn** *then, afterwards*.

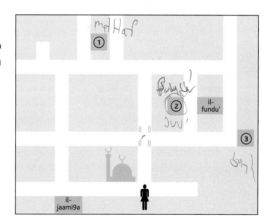

bil 9arabi ...

instructions, e.g. *Go, Take, Turn* are created from the present tense of the verb without its prefixes:

b-aruuH *I go*, **ruuH/ruuHi** *Go* (to m/f)
b-aliff *I turn*, **liff/liffi** *Turn* (to m/f)
b-aakhud *I take*, **khud/khudi** *Take* (to m/f)

Sometimes an **i** or **u** is placed on the front to help with pronunciation: **b-aftaH** *I open*, **iftaH/iftaHi** *Open* (to m/f).   **G14**

3 **2•7** Look at the map again and listen to the directions Sarah is given from the hotel to the university. Which person gives the correct directions?

Making enquiries

1   2•8 Listen to some numbers between 100 and 2,000:

101	**miyya wa waaHid**	500	**khamasmiyya**
102	**miyya wa itnayn**	600	**sittmiyya**
120	**miyya wa 9ishriin**	700	**sab9amiyya**
150	**miyya wa khamsiin**	800	**tamanmiyya**
200	**miitayn**	900	**tis9amiyya**
300	**talatmiyya**	1,000	**alf**
400	**arba9miyya**	2,000	**alfayn**

miyya changes to **mitt** before a noun

2   2•9 Try saying these numbers then listen to check:
130   250   580   634   771   999

3   2•10 Listen to the key language:

huwwa 'ariib/hiyya 'ariiba?	Is it near? (m/f)
huwwa ba9iid/hiyya ba9iida?	Is it far? (m/f)
Hawaali ... min hawn.	It's about ... from here.
... khamasmiit mitr	... 500m
... 9ishriin da'ii'a	... 20 minutes
mumkin taakhudni li ...	Can you take me to ... (to m)

4   2•11 Listen as David Warren takes a taxi to his hotel in the Hamra district of Beirut. You'll hear **ta'riiban** as an alternative to **Hawaali**.

   a   What does the taxi driver say about the Cedarland Hotel?
   b   How long does he say it will take to get there?
   c   How far down **9abd il-9aziiz** Abdel Aziz street is the hotel?

---

bil 9arabi ...

the words for *near* and *far* are **'ariib** and **ba9iid**. They are adjectives so have to agree in gender with what they describe.
il-maktab 'ariib? *Is the office near?*; **laa'**, **il-jaami9a mish 'ariiba.**
No, the university isn't near.   G7

---

5   2•12 David is looking for an internet café. How far away is it?

6   How would you ask the following in Arabic?
   a   Is the market near here?   b   Can you take me to the university?

... and getting help to understand

1   **2•13** Listen to the key language:

mumkin marra taanya? second time	Can you repeat that? *Lit.* possible
mumkin titkallam/ titkallami shway, shway?	Can you speak slowly? (to m/f)
b-titkallam/b-titkallami ingliizi?	Do you speak English? (to m/f)
b-atkallam ingliizi shwayya.	I speak a little English.
maa b-atkallam 9arabi.	I don't speak Arabic.
mish faahim/faahma.	I don't understand. (m/f)

(handwritten: ↳ renew the long vowels, it's real مقام اهم (b))

2   **2•14** In Aleppo Ewan Stewart isn't sure how to get to the **maHaTTat il-qiTaar** *railway station*.

  a   Tick any of the key phrases above that you hear him say.
  b   Where is the railway station?

3   **2•15** While visiting the Roman ruins at Jerash, a Jordanian tries to strike up a conversation with Sarah. Listen and number the dialogue in the order you hear it.

ahlan, ana ismi Abdallah.	7
HaDirtak b-titkallam ingliizi?	4
min wayn HaDirtik?	3
aah, ana faahma! ana min amriika. ismi Sarah.	6
ahlan. min wayn HaDirtik?	1
ahlan fiik. b-atkallam 9arabi shwayya. *(shwayy) coll.*	8
laa', b-atkallam 9arabi bass. ana min il-urdun. min wayn inti?	5
mumkin titkallam shway, shway, law samaHt?	2

> **bil 9arabi ...**
>
> to make a request you can add **mumkin** *possible, can* in front of a verb without the **b-** prefix: **b-aruuH** *I go*; **mumkin aruuH.** *I can go./Can I go?*; **b-titkallam** *you speak*; **mumkin titkallam/ titkallami.** *You can speak./Can you speak?* (to m/f)   **G17**

put it all together

1   Match the Arabic with the English.

a	mumkin marra taanya, min faDlak?	1	Can you speak slowly, please? (to m)
b	mumkin titkallam shway, shway, law samaHt?	2	I speak a little Arabic.
c	b-atkallam 9arabi shwayya.	3	Do you speak English? (to f)
d	maa b-atkallam ingliizi.	4	I don't understand. (f)
e	mish faahma.	5	Could you repeat that, please? (to m)
f	HaDirtik b-titkallami ingliizi?	6	I don't speak English.

2   Fill in the gaps with the words in the box.

khamasmiit   taani   a'rab   aakhir   'ariib   taakhudni   ti'uul li

a   mumkin .... wayn is-suu'?
b   law samaHt, wayn .... Saydaliyya?
c   fiih fundu' fi .... ish-shaari9.
d   fiih maT9am .... min hawn?
e   maktab il-bariid fi .... shaari9 9al-yasaar.
f   mumkin .... lil-jaami9, law samaHt?
g   ta'riiban .... mitr min hawn.

3   Rearrange the following into a conversation:

a   mumkin marra taanya, min faDlak?
b   ruuHi 9ala Tuul, ba9dayn khudi awwal shaari9 9al-yamiin.
c   shukran.
d   laa', mish ba9iid. Hawaali arba9miit mitr min hawn.
e   law samaHt, kiif aruuH lil-matHaf?
f   ruuHi 9ala Tuul, ba9dayn khudi awwal shaari9 9al-yamiin.
g   huwwa ba9iid?

Where does she want to go? What directions is she given? How far away is it?

now you're talking!

1 **2•16** You are in the centre of Damascus and need some directions.

- Say excuse me to a passer-by and ask him where the nearest bank is.
- ◆ **ta'riiban miitayn mitr min hawn 9al-yasaar.**
- You missed that. Ask him to repeat it.
- ◆ **ta'riiban miitayn mitr min hawn 9al-yasaar.**
- Thank him, then say goodbye.
- ◆ **allaah yisalmak.**

2 **2•17** Take the part of Laura Smith, who is lost.

- Stop a passer-by and ask her if she speaks English.
- ◆ **laa', maa b-atkallam ingliizi.**
- Ask her how to get to the railway station from here.
- ◆ **ruuHi 9ala Tuul, ba9dayn khudi taani shaari9 9al-yamiin, wa maHaTTat il-qiTaar fi aakhir ish-shaari9.**
- Say sorry, you don't understand.
- ◆ **ruuHi 9ala Tuul, ba9dayn khudi taani shaari9 9al-yamiin.**
- Repeat the information you've been given, then ask if it's far.
- ◆ **shwayya, mish ba9iida kitiir – ta'riiban kilomitr waaHid min hawn.**
- Thank her.
- ◆ **9afwan.**

quiz

1 Would you turn right or left if someone told you **liff yamiin**?
2 What's the opposite of **'ariib**?
3 Which one of these is not an instruction? **liff, khudi, aruuH**.
4 Which is further **khamasmiit mitr** or **talatmiit mitr**?
5 How would you ask a man to repeat something?
6 What does **shway, shway** mean?
7 How would a woman say *I'm sorry, I don't know*.
8 What do you think **maa b-atkallam fransi** means?

Now check whether you can ...

- ask where a place is and how to get there
- follow some basic directions
- understand distances
- ask someone to repeat what they've said and to speak more slowly
- check if someone speaks English
- say you speak a little Arabic
- say you don't know or understand
- count to 2,000

Practise what you've learnt in this unit by using **wayn** and **kiif aruuH** to ask where the places are you learnt in Unit 5, and how you'd get to them. Then have a go at counting in Arabic without looking at the book.

Arabic script: 7

1   Look at the following two letters:

Letter	Sound	Isolated	Final	Medial	Initial
faa	f	ف	ـف	ـفـ	فـ
qaaf	q or '	ق	ـق	ـقـ	قـ

2   Match the following foods which all contain the letter **faa**:

1 fuul   2 kunaafa   3 falaafil   4 kufta   5 filfil *pepper*

a كنافة   b فلفل   c كفتة   d فلافل   e فول

The **qaaf** is pronounced as a **q** in MSA but in Egypt and parts of the Levant it is pronounced as a glottal stop in everyday words such as:
'ahwa قهوة *coffee*; **'amiiS** قميص *shirt*.

You will hear the **qaaf** pronounced as a **q** even in spoken Egyptian and Levantine Arabic in more sophisticated words such as:
al-qaahira القاهرة *Cairo*; **al-qur'aan** القرآن *The Qur'an*.

Written Arabic	Spoken Levant and Egypt	MSA	Meaning
قهوة	'ahwa	qahwa	*coffee*
قميص	'amiiS	qamiiS	*shirt*
أزرق	azra'	azraq	*blue*

3   Do you know what these signs mean? Where might you see them?

1 مقفول   2 مفتوح

4   Match the following words:

1 maHaTTa   5 suuq
2 funduq   6 ghurfa
3 maSr   7 matHaf
4 baqqaal

a متحف   e غرفة
b بقال   f محطة
c فندق   g مصر
d سوق

Check your answers on page 90.

Arabic script: the hamza

The **hamza** is a letter which looks like a small hat **ء**. It has the sound of a silent cough or a glottal stop similar to the Cockney wa'er (water). There are rules for how it is used depending on where it appears in a word:

- At the beginning of a word the **hamza** always appears on or below an **alif**, and is known as **alif hamza**.
  If the initial **hamza** is followed by **a** or **u** then it sits on the **alif أ**.
  If the initial **hamza** is followed by **i** then it sits below the **alif إ**.
  In colloquial Arabic you rarely see the **hamza** represented in the transliteration.

1 Match the following words which begin with **alif hamza**:

1 ana   2 ismi   3 ukhti   4 abi   5 ummi   6 akhi

إسمي e أبي d أخي c أنا b أمي a أختي

- In certain circumstances the **hamza** is omitted from the beginning of a word altogether. The most common example is when the definite article **il- الـ** *the* is used. You will notice this on signs:
  il-qaahira القاهرة *Cairo*; **il-wuSuul الوصول** *arrivals*

- At the end of a word the **hamza** sometimes sits on its own on the line. This can be clearly seen in the feminine form of colours:
  sayyaara Hamra   سيارة حمراء *red car*

2 Match the following feminine colours, all of which end with the **hamza** sitting on its own on the line:

1 bayDa ○   4 Safra ○

2 sawda ●   5 zar'a ●

3 khaDra ○

a سوداء   d زرقاء
b خضراء   e بيضاء
c صفراء

3 Can you recognise this famous Arab city which ends with a **hamza**?

الدار البيضاء

Check your answers on page 90.

'addaysh haada? *kam haada*

asking for what you want

understanding the price

shopping in a market

bargaining

There are many different currencies throughout the Arab world, the main ones being: **dirham**: Morocco and UAE; **gineeh** *pound:* Egypt and Sudan; **lira** *pound*: Syria and Lebanon; **dinaar**: Algeria, Bahrain, Kuwait, Tunisia, Libya, Jordan and Iraq; **riyaal**: Saudi Arabia, Qatar and Oman. The *British pound* is referred to as **gineeh isterliini** as opposed to **gineeh maSri** for the *Egyptian pound*.

Prices are normally fixed in shops, but bargaining is the custom in the **suu'** regardless of whether the customer is Arab or non-Arab. Bargaining is part of the culture and can be very enjoyable and usually both customer and seller are happy with the end result.

The symbol for the Egyptian pound is £E. The various symbols for **lira suuriyya** *Syrian pound* are £S, S£, SP, and L.S.

lubnaniyya

Asking for what you want

(handwritten: ʾabʿaS Cymk   ḥiṣa   mee badi)

1   2•18 Listen to the key language:

mumkin ashuuf …	Can I have a look at …
… haada-l 'amiiS.	… this/that shirt (m).
… haadi-sh shanTa.	… this/that bag (f).
… ma'aas akbar?	… a larger size?
mumkin a'iisu/a'iisha?	Can I try it on? (m/f)
kibiir/kibiira (shwayya).	It's (too) big. (m/f)
Saghiir/Saghiira (shwayya).	It's (too) small. (m/f)

---

bil 9arabi …

adjectives follow nouns and agree with them in gender and use of
the definite article: 'amiiS kibiir *a big shirt* (m); il-'amiiS il-kibiir
the big shirt. Lit. *the shirt the big*. For most colours the feminine is
formed by removing the a- from the beginning of the masculine
and placing it at the end: akhDar/khaDra *green* (m/f); 'amiiS
akhDar *a green shirt*; ish-shanTa il-khaDra *the green bag*.   **G7**

2   2•19 Linda wants to buy an **isharb** *scarf* from the Hamidiyyeh Market
in Damascus. You'll hear **alwaan taanya** meaning *other colours*. *(handwritten: lawn-colour ألوان)*

aHmar/Hamra ■	akhDar/khaDra ■	azra'/zar'a ■
aswad/sawda ■	aSfar/Safra ✗	abyaD/bayDa □

Listen to the conversation and circle the colours you hear mentioned.

3   2•20 Ewan Stewart sees a shirt he likes in a Beirut shop window.
Listen and decide which statements are TRUE or FALSE:
a   he wants a blue shirt   *(handwritten: ✗ أزرق)*
b   the shirt is too small   *(handwritten: ✓)*
c   there isn't a large size   *(handwritten: ✓)*

4   2•21 Amal Ayyoubi is in Marrakesh and wants to buy a handbag.
Listen to the dialogue and complete the extracts below.
Which **lawn** *colour* does Amal think is **Hilu/Hilwa**
pretty (m/f)?

● mumkin ashuuf haadi-sh shanTa …… *(iz-zar'a)* ?

◆ b-tHibbi haadi-sh shanTa … *(il-Hamra)* ?

● laa', maa b-aHibb il-lawn …… *(il-aHmar)* …

◆ shuufi haadi-sh shanTa …… *(il-khaDra)* …

il-aHmar
il-Hamra
il-khaDra
iz-zar'a

Understanding the price

1   2•22 Listen to the key language:

'addaysh ...   How much is/are ...
... hadawl?   ... these/those?
... hadawl il-kuruut?   ... these postcards?
hadawl bi miyya wa saba9iin dinar.   Those are 170 dinars.
haada ghaali/haadi ghaalya (kitiir). It's (very) expensive. (m/f)
9andak/9andik shi arkhaS?   Do you have anything
                                      cheaper? (to m/f)

---

bil 9arabi ...

to make comparisons first remove the vowels from the adjective.
With **kibiir** *big* this leaves you the root letters **k b r**, to which you
add **a** at the beginning and after the second root letter: **akbar**
bigger/biggest. There's no separate feminine form: **Saghiir** *small*,
aSghar *smaller/smallest*; **rakhiiS** *cheap*, **arkhaS** *cheaper/cheapest*.

The comparative, e.g. *bigger* comes after the noun: **ma'aas akbar**
a bigger size. The superlative e.g. *biggest* comes before the noun,
as in English, but it does not require the definite article *the*: **akbar
ma'aas** *the biggest size*.   **G21**

---

2   2•23 Farida is on a trip to Amman and is asking the prices of various
    items in a clothes shop. Listen and write in the prices for the following:

a bluuza   **b fustaan**   **c jakayt**

3   Why is the dress so expensive?

4   2•24 Mark Jones wants to buy a few things from the **kushk** *kiosk* next
    to his hotel. Listen and note which items match the prices below:

    a £E20   **b** £E80   **c** £E90   **d** £E200

---

jariida/jaraa'id *newspaper(s)* **majalla/majallaat** *magazine(s)* **kitaab/
kutub** *book(s)* **Taabi9/Tawaabi9** *stamp(s)* **kart/kuruut** *postcard(s)*

Which item is not available? Where is he told to go?

5   How would you say:
    ● This bag is very expensive. ● How much are these books?

Shopping in a market

1   2•25 Listen to the key language:

mumkin ashuufu?	Can I see it? (m)
mumkin ashuufha?	Can I see it (f)/them?
'addaysh biddak/biddik?	How many do you want? (to m/f)
b-aakhud ...	I'll have *Lit*. I take ...
... haada/haadi.	... this one. (m/f)
... hadawl/khamsa min hadawl.	... these/five of these.
b-aakhdu.	I'll take it. (m)
b-aakhudha.	I'll take it (f)/them.
biddak/biddik shi taani?	Would you like anything else? (to m/f)

2   2•26 Linda is visiting Aleppo's famous covered market. You'll hear a shopkeeper telling her what she might find. Tick the items you hear. Listen out for **laakin** *but* and **mumtaaz/mumtaaza** *excellent* (m/f).

tawaabil *spices*		**SaHn/SuHuun** *large dish(es)*
finjaan/fanaajiin *cup(s)*		**ibrii' shaay** *tea pot*
Siniyya/Sawaani *tray(s)*		**ibrii' 'ahwa** *coffee pot*

finjaan ahv

3   2•27 Linda is at another stall and asks about two items. Which ones does she ask for? What does she buy? Listen out for **bass** which in this context means *only*.

4   2•28 In Damascus Mark Jones wants to buy some traditional **fukhaar** *earthenware* in the Hamidiyyeh Market. Listen and write in the quantity of each item he asks for:

cups .... dishes .... coffee pots ....

---

bil 9arabi ...

because nouns are either masculine or feminine, you use *him* and *her* for the English *it*. *Him* is translated by adding **-u** to the verb, *her* by adding **-ha**:

b-aakhdu *I'll take it* (m); **b-aakhudha** *I'll take it* (f)
a'iisu *I try it on* (m); **a'iisha** *I try it on* (f)

-ha is also used for *them* when referring to inanimate objects of either gender: **b-aakhudha** *I'll take them*.

[handwritten top margin: mushkila – problem / مشكلة ← mish]

Bargaining

1   **2•29** Listen to the key language:

biddi ashuuf bass. — I'm just looking. *Lit.* I want I look only.
biddi ashtiri ... — I want to buy ...
shuu aHsan taman _[Arabic: ثمن]_ — What's your best price? (to m/f)
9andak/9andik?
miitayn lira mniiH? — Is 200 Syrian pounds OK?
mish mumkin. — It's not possible.

2   **2•30** Sarah Walker joins Mark at the market and sees a coffee pot she likes. Listen and make a note of:

a the original price in Syrian pounds .... _[handwritten: 50 → 275]_
b how much she agrees on after some hard bargaining .... _[handwritten: 250]_

3   **2•30** Listen again. Did you hear how the shopkeeper agreed to Sarah's final price?

Note it down in English and Arabic. ....

---

bil 9arabi ...

there is no infinitive e.g. *to buy, to drink*. You literally say *I want I buy, you want you buy* etc: **biddi ashtiri** *I want to buy* Lit. *I want I buy*; **biddak tishtiri** *you want to buy* Lit. *you want you buy.*

---

4   **2•31** Mark continues his stroll around the market and a vendor attracts his attention. Listen to the dialogue and fill in the gaps with the words in the box:

● itfaDDal, itfaDDal, ya akhi. shuu biddak ..._[tishtiri]_...?
◆ biddi ..._[ashuuf]_.... bass.
● haada-S SaHn jamiil kitiir.
◆ laa', shukran, maa biddi ..._[ashtiri]_...
● iS-Siniyya bi miitayn lira bass!
◆ miyya wa khamsiin lira ..._[mniiH]_...?
● laa', mish mumkin.
◆ shuu ..._[aHsan]_... taman 9andak?
● miyya wa saba9iin lira.
◆ ..._[b-aakhudha]_ _[eg]_...

[speech bubble]
jamiil/jamiila
beautiful (m/f)

[box:] mniiH   ashtiri   b-aakhudha
ashuuf   tishtiri   aHsan

put it all together

1 Which is the odd one out? Why?

   a bluuza, 'amiiS, isharb, Siniyya

   b rakhiiS, akbar, aSghar, aghla

   c dinaar, gineeh, dirham, miyya

   d abyaD, aswad, akbar, azra'

2 Fill in the gaps with the words in the box.

   | arkhaS | il-aswad | akbar | mumtaaz |
   | il-Hilwa | iz-zar'a | kibiir | il-aHmar |

   a 'addaysh ish-shanTa _____? (blue)

   b b-aakhud haada-l isharb _____ (black)

   c biddi ashtiri il-bluuza _____ (pretty)

   d il-jakayt _____ kitiir. (big)

   e mumkin a'iis il-fustaan _____? (red)

   f mumkin ashuuf _____ ibrii' 'ahwa 9andak? (biggest)

   g 9andik 'amiiS _____? (cheaper)

   h haada-l kitaab _____ (excellent)

3 Choose the correct option for each sentence from the pair given below.

   a b-aHibb iS-SaHn. mumkin _____?

   b biddi _____ khamsa min hadawl.

   c haadi-S Siniyya Hilwa kitiir. _____.

   d 9andik _____ fustaan lawn akhDar?

   e it-tawaabil mumtaaza. _____

   f 'addaysh _____ fanaajiin?

a ashuufu/ashuufa	b ashtiri/tishtiri
c b-aakhdu/b-aakhudha	d haadi-l/haada-l
e b-aakhdu/b-aakhudha	f haada-l/hadawl il-

now you're talking!

1   **2•32** Imagine you're visiting Aleppo and doing a bit of shopping in the **suu'**.

- **ahlan, SabaaH il-khayr.**
- ◆ Reply, and ask how much the white shirt is.
- **il-'amiiS bi miyya wa 9ishriin lira.**
- ◆ Ask if you can try it on.
- **itfaDDal.**
- ◆ Say it's a bit small. Ask if he has a larger size.
- **laa', maa 9andi.**

2   **2•33** Now you're looking for a leather handbag for your sister. You'll hear **itfaDDal** meaning *come this way*.

- **marHaba, ahlan wa sahlan. itfaDDal.**
- ◆ Say excuse me, and ask the woman how much this handbag is.
- **haadi bi tis9amiit lira suuriyya.**
- ◆ Ask if she has the bag in red.
- **9andi bass aswad wa azra'.**
- ◆ Say OK, you'll take the blue bag.

3   **2•34** Now for some souvenirs. You'll hear **kwayyis** *good*.

- **aywa, ayy khidma?**
- ◆ Ask if you could have a look at this tray.
- **itfaDDal.**
- ◆ Ask how much it is.
- **haadi bi miitayn lira.**
- ◆ Say that it's very expensive. Ask if 120 is ok.
- **laa', mish mumkin.**
- ◆ Ask what his best price is.
- **miyya wa sittiin kwayyis?**
- ◆ Offer 150 Syrian pounds.
- **Tayyib, itfaDDal.**

quiz

1 What's the difference between **iS-SaHn jamiil** and **iS-SaHn il-jamiil**?

2 Which is more: **miitayn riyaal** or **itnayn riyaal**?

3 Change the word **Tawiil** *tall* to *taller*.

4 Which word means *many* and *very*?

5 What does the word **lawn** mean?

6 How would you say *I would like five of those*?

7 Which of these phrases means *the smallest shirt*? **'amiiS aSghar; aSghar 'amiiS**.

8 What is the feminine of the colour **aHmar**?

9 How do you say *I'll take them*?

10 If **alwaan taanya** means *other colours*, how would you say *other postcards*?

Now check whether you can:

- ask how much something costs
- understand currencies used in the Arab World
- ask for an item in a shop
- ask if you can look at something
- ask if you can try something on
- explain that something is too big, small or expensive
- ask for a smaller/bigger size
- ask for different colours
- bargain on a price

Word association can double the amount of vocabulary you retain. For example, you could link in your mind words in similar categories, such as **kart** and **Taabi9**, or **shaay** and **'ahwa**. When you learn an adjective, learn any obvious opposite as well: **kibiir** and **Saghiir**, **rakhiiS** and **ghaali**.

Checkpoint 2

1   **2•35** You ask the receptionist at the Cedarland Hotel in Beirut about visiting three places you need to get to. Listen and make a note of where each one is and how long it would take to get there from the hotel.

		where?	how far?
a	**maT9am kababji** *Kababji Restaurant*	....	....
b	**il-jaami9a il-amriikiyya** *The American University*	....	....
c	**il-matHaf il-waTani** *The National Museum*	....	....

2   **2•36** You now need to know which days these three places are open. Listen to the receptionist and fill in the table:

	Open	Closed
maT9am kababji		
il-jaami9a il-amriikiyya		
il-matHaf il-waTani		

3   Select which phrase you might use:

1 **wayn a'rab maT9am?**

2 **huwwa ba9iid?**

3 **ana aasif/asfa.**

4 **mumkin ashuuf haada?**

5 **9andak ma'aas akbar?**

6 **HaDirtak b-titkallim ingliizi?**

7 **mumkin a'iis?**

8 **'addaysh haada?**

9 **haada ghaali kitiir.**

10 **mumkin marra taanya, min faDlak?**

a to find out if someone speaks English. b to ask to try something on.
c to ask where the nearest restaurant is. d to ask for a larger size.
e to ask if you can look at something. f to say that it's very expensive.
g to get someone to repeat what they have said. h to ask how much something costs.
i to say you are sorry. j to ask if somewhere is far.

4 Group the following words into seven groups of three words.

mi'aabil   ruuH   finjaan   9ala Tuul   isharb
maktab bariid   arba9miyya   Siniyya   liff
janb   'amiiS   talatmiyya   maHaTTa
9al-yasaar   9al-yamiin   matHaf   ibrii'
miitayn   fustaan   waraa   khud

5 Find the correct word to make a match

a finjaan   1 aHmar
b jariida   2 zar'a
c shanTa   3 il-bariid
d maHaTTat   4 il-madiina
e maktab   5 shaay
f wasaT   6 il-qiTaar
g fustaan   7 ingliiziyya

6 2•37 Listen to the prices for the following items in a Syrian **suu'** and
   write them down.

	L.S.
coffee pot	
English newspaper	
6 cups	
Arabic tray	
shirt	
scarf	

7 Which questions would you ask to receive the following answers?

a .... aywa, b-atkallam ingliizi shwayya.

b .... a'rab Saydaliyya khamsamiit mitr
                                                min hawn.

c .... laa', il-maHaTTa ba9iida min hawn.

d .... il-bank maftuuH min is-saa9a tis9a
                                                lis-saa9a waaHda.

e .... haada bi sittiin dinaar.

f .... maa fiih suubermarket hawn.

8 Fill the gaps in these sentences using the words in the box:

1 **haadi-S Siniyya** .... **kitiir.**

2 **miitayn wa khamsiin lira** ....?

3 **mumkin** .... **haada-l fustaan, law samaHti?**

4 **shuu** .... **taman?**

5 .... **aruuH lil-maHaTTa?**

6 **ruuH 9ala Tuul wa ba9dayn** .... **yamiin.**

7 .... **awwal shaari9 9al-yasaar.**

aHsan	kiif	ghaalya	a'iis	liff	mniiH	khud

9 **2·38** Listen to four people being given directions from Café France in Casablanca. Follow their route on the map and write down in English the place they're going to and the number which corresponds to it on the map. You'll hear **na9am**, which is another way of saying *yes*.

1 ....   2 ....

3 ....   4 ....

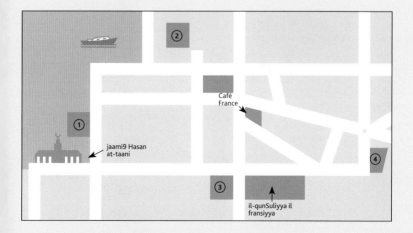

10 Complete the descriptions next to each pair of items using an appropriate word from the list. Here **min** means *than*.

   a aSghar   b akbar   c aghla   d arkhaS

1 il-fustaan il-azra' .... min il-fustaan il-aHmar.

2 ish-shanTa il-Hamra .... min ish-shanTa il-khaDra.

3 is-sayyaara il-bayDa .... min is-sayyaara iz-zar'a.

4 il-kitaab il-aswad ....min il-kitaab il-aSfar.

11 Look at this shopping list. Put 1 by the ones you would buy in a **ba'aal**; 2 in a **kushk** and 3 in a **suu'**

  a majalla ☐   b tuffaaH ☐   c fanaajiin ☐

  d Siniyya ☐   e jariida ☐   f burtu'aan ☐

  g ibrii' 'ahwa ☐   h shammaam ☐   i kuruut ☐

9andak ghurfa?

finding a suitable hotel room

... and saying how long you want to stay

checking in at the hotel

making requests

In the Arab world there's a wide range of hotels which are generally known as **fundu'**, although the word **utiil** is used in many Arab countries as well.

Hotels range from small family run outfits to the most luxurious **saba9 nujuum** *seven-star* hotels of Dubai. Breakfast in the smaller hotels is normally French style, particularly in Egypt, North Africa and the Levant. Staying in the older ex-colonial type of hotel in the Arab world can be delightful but it's advisable to check whether the room has **takyiif** *air-conditioning* in the summer months as not all rooms are equipped with this.

Guests will often be asked to leave their **jawaaz safar** *passport* at reception overnight as visitors need to be registered with the local police and this is normally done by the hotel.

Finding a suitable hotel room

1   2•39 Listen to the key language:

9andak/9andik ghurfa?	Do you have a room? (to m/f)
biddi ghurfa li shakhS waaHid/	I want a room for one person/
li shakhSayn.	for two people.
bi Hammaam/fuTuur/	with a bathroom/breakfast/
takyiif	air-conditioning
li kam shakhS?	For how many people?
li talaat ashkhaaS.	For three people.
'addaysh il-layla?	How much is it a night?
il-layla bi miyya wa khamsiin lira.	It's 150 Syrian pounds per
	night.

---

bil 9arabi ...

to say *two* of something, a special form called the dual is used.
It's made by adding **-ayn** onto the end of the noun. If the noun
ends with **-a** then **-tayn** is added: **shakhS** *a person*, **shakh**<u>**Sayn**</u>
two people; **layla** *a night*, **lay**<u>**ltayn**</u> *two nights.* The dual form is
not used when ordering food or drinks.   **G20**

---

2   2•40 Listen to some people asking about rooms at the Baron Hotel in
Aleppo. Tick what kind of accommodation they want.

Sami Ayyoub					
Sonya Brett					
Mohammed Bakry					
Miriam Haddad					

3   2•41 Listen as Sami now enquires about the prices. Jot down what the
price is per night with and without breakfast.

... and saying how long you want to stay

1 **2•42** Listen to the key language:

li kam layla?	For how many nights?
biddi anzil ...	I want to stay for ...
... layltayn/talaat layaali/	... two nights/three nights/
haadi-l layla bass.	just tonight *Lit.* this night only.
aymta biddak tinzil/biddik tinzili?	When do you want to stay?
(to m/f)	
min il-yawm li yawm it-talaata	from today until Tuesday
min yawm waaHid sitta li	from the 1st of June to the 3rd
talaata sitta	of June
aasif/asfa, il-fundu' kullu	Sorry (m/f), the hotel is
maHjuuz.	full.

2 **2•43** Listen as guests say how long they want to stay at the Sham Palace Hotel in Damascus. From the list below number the three you hear in the order you hear them:

haadi-l layla bass   3

talaat layaali

min il-yawm li yawm it-talaata 2

min il-yawm li yawm il-jum9a

layltayn   1

---

bil 9arabi ...

the names for months can differ from region to region in the Arabic-speaking world. It is becoming increasingly common to hear numbers being used instead. The number of the day comes first, followed directly by the number of the month: **yawm waaHid sitta** *1 June* Lit. *day 1/6*; **yawm tis9a 9ashara** *9 October* Lit. *day 9/10*. These can also mean *on 1 June, on 9 October*.

---

3 **2•44** The receptionist at the Ummayad Hotel is taking some bookings over the phone. Listen and note when the three callers want rooms. Which caller cannot be accommodated?

a ....1........ b ....2.... c 4/5 6/9

1/6 3/6

Checking in at the hotel

1   **2•45** Listen to the key language:

9andi Hajz.	I have a reservation.
Hajazt/Hajazti aymta?	When did you book? (to m/f)
Hajazt imbaariH.	I booked yesterday.
jawaaz safarak/safarik,	Please give me your passport.
min faDlak/min faDlik.	(to m/f)
imla/imli il-istimaara,	Please fill in the form. (to m/f)
min faDlak/min faDlik.	
itfaDDal/itfaDDali il-muftaaH.	Here's your key. (to m/f)
il-asinsiir fiT-Taabi' il-awwal/	The lift is on the first/second/
it-taani/it-taalit.	third <u>floor</u>.

---

bil 9arabi ...

the past tense uses suffixes which are added to the verb, as opposed to prefixes, which are used in the present tense: <u>a</u>Hjiz *I book,* **Hajaz<u>t</u>** *I booked.* **<u>ti</u>Hjiz** *you book* (m), **Hajaz<u>t</u>** *you booked* (m). **<u>ti</u>Hjiz<u>i</u>** *you book* (f), **Hajaz<u>ti</u>** *you booked* (f).   **G9–11**

---

2   **2•46** Listen to a visitor checking in the Sindibad Hotel in Rabat and tick the correct options. You'll hear **ghurfa raqm** *room number.*

  a She's booked a ▪ single ▪ double ▪ double with bath
  b She's staying for ▪ two nights ▪ three nights ▪ four nights
  c She's asked ▪ for her passport ▪ to fill in the form
      ▪ if she wants breakfast
  d Her room number is ▪ 110 ▪ 220 ▪ 210

3   **2•46** Listen again, what was the problem with her booking?

4   **2•47** Listen to someone else checking in, and complete the details of their booking on the form opposite. Then listen again to find out:

  a which floor the room on
  b where the lift is.

ism: ....
min: .... li: ....
jawaaz raqm: ....
jinsiyya: ....
ghurfa raqm: ....

Making requests

1   **2•48** Listen to the key language:

mumkin ...	Can ...
... **akhalli shanTati hawn?**	... I leave my suitcase here?
... **adfa9 bi haada-l kart?**	... I pay with this card?
... **asta9mil Hammaam is-sibaaHa?**	... I use the swimming pool?
... **ashuuf il-mudiir?**	... I see the manager?
... **tuTlub/tuTlubi taksi 9ashaani?**	... you order a taxi for me?
(to m/f)	
akiid	certainly

[al\`o; an akiid]

2   **2•49** Maryam Munir is about to check out of the Sindibad Hotel.
Listen to what she says to the receptionist Hasan Abaaza and make a
note in English of the two things she asks for:

a ....   b ....

What do you think **ayy khidma taanya** means?

---

bil 9arabi ...

mumkin is used with the present tense without the **b**-prefix. As well
as being used to mean *Can I?* as in **mumkin adfa9?** *Can I pay?*
it is also used when politely asking someone to do something:
mumkin tuTlub/tuTlubi ...? *Can you order/request ...?* (to m/f)
mumkin ti'uul li/ti'uuli li ...? *Can you tell me ...?* (to m/f).   **G17**

---

3   **2•50** The guests are keeping Hasan Abaaza busy with their requests.
Listen and match the guests with what they want.

Mrs Campbell	use the swimming pool
Dr Rushdi	leave his suitcase here
Mr Ramzi	see the manager
Miss Buthayna	pay with this card

4   **2•50** Listen to the conversations again. Which request could Hasan
Abaaza not agree to? Why not?

put it all together

Hajazt imbaariH.	bi takyiif
9andi Hajz.	'addaysh il-layla?
9andik ghurfa?	biddi anzil haadi-l layla bass.
mumkin asta9mil Hammaam is-sibaaHa?	

1   Which phrase from the box would you use to:

   a   ask if there's a room available

   b   say with air-conditioning

   c   say you want to stay tonight only

   d   say you have a reservation

   e   ask the price per night

   f   ask if you can use the swimming pool

   g   say you booked yesterday

2   Complete the following:

   a   **9andak ghurfa li** ………………… **?**

   b   **biddi ghurfa li** …………… **bi** ……………

   c   **biddi ghurfa bi** …………………

   d   **mumkin** ………… …………… **9ashaani?**

   e   **mumkin** ………… ………… **?**

3   Say these dates in Arabic:

   a   31 January   **b**   24 December

   c   5 March   **d**   8 July

now you're talking!

1   **2•51** You're at the Shepheard's Hotel in Amman looking for a room for one night.

- **marHaba, ayy khidma?**
- ◆ Ask if they have a room available.
- **biddak tinzil li kam layla?**
- ◆ Say for one night only.
- **li shakhS waaHid?**
- ◆ Say no, say you want a double with a bathroom.
- **aywa, fiih ghurfa bi saba9iin dinaar il-layla.**
- ◆ Ask if breakfast is included.
- **aywa, bi fuTuur.**

2   **2•52** The following morning you're ready to check out.

- **SabaaH il-khayr.**
- ◆ Say good morning to her.
- **ayy khidma?**
- ◆ Ask for the bill.
- **raqm il-ghurfa, law samaHt?**
- ◆ Say you're in room 210.
- **saba9iin dinaar, min faDlak.**
- ◆ Ask if you can pay with this card.
- **aywa, Tab9an.**
- ◆ Ask if you can leave your suitcase there until 4 o'clock today.
- **aywa, akiid. b-ashuufak ba9dayn.**
- ◆ Say goodbye.

quiz

1 Which is the odd one out? **layla**, **yawm**, **layltayn**, **ghurfa**.

2 In a hotel how would you say *I want to stay for four nights*?

3 What is the Arabic for *7 October*?

4 Who is **il-mudiir** in a hotel?

5 How would say *a room with air-conditioning*?

6 Would you use **mumkin tuTlubi taksi 9ashaani?** or **mumkin tuTlub taksi 9ashaani?** to ask a man to call a taxi for you?

7 What do you do if you hear **imla il-istimaara**?

8 If you're given **il-muftaaH** what do you have?

9 How would you ask for two rooms?

Now check whether you can ...

- ask if there's a room available
- specify what kind of room, with bathroom/breakfast/air-conditioning
- ask how much it costs per night
- say how long you want accommodation for, giving precise dates
- say you've booked a room
- ask if you can do something, e.g. leave your suitcase
- ask someone to do something for you

When learning a language it can be easy to underestimate how much you know. Go back to the early units to prove to yourself how much you've learnt. Think also about what you find easy ... and difficult. If you can identify your strengths and weaknesses, you can shape your own learning.

Arabic script: numbers

Many Arab countries outside North Africa use written numerals known as the Hindi or Persian numerals. These read from left to right as in English and are as follows.

0	1	2	3	4	5	6	7	8	9	10
٠	١	٢	٣	٤	٥	٦	٧	٨	٩	١٠

1 Can you read the distances in kilometres كم of the following places as marked on the Damascus-Aleppo Motorway?

airport ....

Homs ....

Hama ....

Aleppo ....

المطار ٢٦ كم ✈

حمص ٢١٠ كم

حمـاة ٣٣٠ كم

حلــب ٤٤٦ كم

2 You have been given a business card by Nabil Nisnaas. Write in English the telephone numbers, which are presented on the card in the following order:

1 home

....

2 office

....

3 mobile

....

الاسم : نبيل نسناس

رقم التلفون: البيت: ٠٥٣٣٢٨٦٢٨٤٤

المكتب: ٠٥٣٣١٧٤٦١٦١

الموبيل: ٠٦٢٥٧١٨٨٩٩٢

Check your answers on page 90.

Arabic script: answers

Arabic script: 1

2

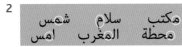

انا البيت بريطانيا
امس سيارة عمان

3 *1 c, I / I am; 2 f, daughter/girl;*
3 e, father; 4 b, my son; 5 d, door,
gate; 6 g, girls; 7 a, two

Arabic script: 2

2

مكتب سلام شمس
محطة المغرب امس

3 salaam *peace*
4 *1 b, king; 2 c, sun; 3 a, office; 4 d,*
book

Arabic script: 3

2

مدرسة سيارة يسار
رقم عربي

Right to left: madrasa *school,*
sayyaara *car,* yasaar *left,* raqm
number, 9arabi *Arabic*

3 *1 f; 2 h; 3 e; 4 g; 5 d; 6 b; 7 a; 8 c*
4 *1 d; 2 e; 3 b; 4 c; 5 a*
5 *1* as-suudaan *Sudan; 2* suuriya
Syria.

Arabic script: 4

2

هناك هذه سهل
مهندس هذا اسمه

3 *1 d; 2 a; 3 b; 4 c*
4 *1 e; 2 a; 3 d*

Arabic script: 5

2

مطار طلب مطعم
قطار فطور

Right to left: maTaar *airport,*
Talab *request,* maT9am
restaurant, qiTaar *train,* fuTuur
breakfast

3 *Abu Dhabi*
4 *1 10.40; 2 Rabat; 3 departing;*
4 no

Arabic script: 6

2

عندي شارع مصنع
عمل نعم مطعم

3 shaay bi na9na9 *d;* 9aSiir 9inab *c*
4 *1 c; 2 a; 3 d; 4 b*
5 *3 is correct. 1* shaari9 lubnaan; *2*
shaari9 9abd al-9aziiz; *4* shaari9
il-Hamra

Arabic script: 7

2 *1 e; 2 a; 3 d; 4 c; 5 b*
3 *On shop doors. 1* maqfuul *closed;*
2 maftuuH *open.*
4 *1 f; 2 c; 3 g; 4 b; 5 d; 6 e; 7 a*

The hamza

1 *1 c; 2 f; 3 a; 4 e; 5 b; 6 d*
2 *1 e; 2 a; 3 b; 4 c; 5 d*
3 id-daar il-bayDa *Casablanca*

Numbers

1 *Airport 26km; Homs 210km;*
Hama 330km; Aleppo 446km
2 *House: 05332862844; office:*
05331746161; mobile: 0625
7188992

fiih qiTaar li Halab?

saying where you're going

asking about public transport

buying tickets

checking travel times

The majority of foreign visitors to the Arab world use public transport to travel between cities. For travel within cities use taxis; they're great places to practise your Arabic!

qiTaaraat *trains* are generally clean, efficient and inexpensive as they're often government owned. Networks vary in size and in some Arab countries there is virtually no network at all. Generally **daraja uula** *first class* is good value as it is usually air-conditioned and refreshments are available.

To explore scenic parts of Arab countries not served by public transport you can take a **sayyaara mu'ajjara** *hire car*. You can often get a better rate locally but you need to make sure prices include **ta'miin** *insurance*.

Saying where you're going

1   **2•53** Listen to the key language:

biddi aruuH li ba9albak il-yawm.	I want to go to Baalbek today.
raayiH/raayHa lil-maTaar bukra.	I'm going to the airport tomorrow. (m/f)
HaDirtak raayiH/HaDirtik raayHa aymta?	When are you going? (to m/f)
laazim taakhud/taakhdi taksi.	You must take a taxi. (to m/f)
mumkin aakhud il-qiTaar?	Can I take the train?
mumkin tiruuH/tiruuHi ...	You can go ... (to m/f)
... bil baaS/bil qiTaar.	... by bus/by train.

bil 9arabi ...

raayiH/raayHa (m/f) *going* is an active participle like saakin/ saakna *living* (see page 20). It's used a lot in spoken Arabic, and in the Levant is followed by the preposition li.   **G12**

2   **2•54** A guest at the Safir Hotel in Beirut is asking the receptionist about different ways to get to Baalbek. You will hear **qiTaaraat** *trains*.

Tick the modes of transport which are available:

3   **2•55** A visitor to Amman asks how he can get from his hotel to the airport. Listen and number their conversation in the order you hear it.

raayiH lil maTaar bukra. mumkin aakhud il-baaS min hawn?
Hawaali arba9iin dinaar.
SabaaH in-nuur.
laa', maa fiih baaS lil-maTaar. laazim taakhud taksi.
'addaysh it-taksi min hawn lil-maTaar?
haada ghaali kitiir!
SabaaH il-khayr.

4   How would you say the following?
- I want to go to the museum.
- Can I take the bus?

Asking about public transport

1 **2•56** Listen to the key language:

haada-l baaS b-yruuH li 9ammaan?	Does this bus go to Amman?
min wayn b-yruuH?	Where does it go from?
ayy raqm baaS?	Which number bus?
'addaysh b-yaakhud?	How long does it take? (m)
'addaysh b-taakhud ir-riHla?	How long does the journey take? (f)
b-yaakhud/b-taakhud ...	It takes ... (m/f)
... saa9a waaHda/saa9atayn.	... 1 hour/2 hours.
... arba9a saa9aat.	... 4 hours.

---

bil 9arabi ...

yaakhud *to take* is used when talking about the time something takes. The masculine **b-yaakhud** is used in a general sense: **b-yaakhud 9ashar da'aayi'** *it takes 10 minutes*; while the feminine **b-taakhud** is used when referring to a specific feminine noun: **ir-riHla b-taakhud ...** *the journey (f) takes ...*   **G1, G20**

---

2   **2•57** Linda is at the **maHaTTat il-baaSaat** *bus station* in Damascus. Listen and decide whether the following statements are true or false.

	True	False
a This bus is going to the university.		
b No. 32 bus goes to the Umayyad Mosque.		
c The journey takes twenty minutes.		
d There isn't a bus to the airport from here.		

3   **2•58** Linda is going to go on some long-distance bus journeys. Listen and write down how long they take. You'll hear **hunaak** *over there*.

a Damascus-Aleppo ....

b Damascus-Amman ....

c Damascus-Homs ....

4   **2•58** Listen again and note down where the buses to Aleppo and Homs go from.

Buying tickets

1 **2•59** Listen to the key language:

biddi tazkartayn li dimashq,	I'd like two tickets for
min faDlak/min faDlik.	Damascus, please. (to m/f)
daraja <u>uula</u>/daraja <u>taanya</u>	<u>first</u>/<u>second</u> class
ruuHa	single
ruuHa raj9a	return
tazkarat ruuHa raj9a	a return ticket
ayy raSiif?	Which platform?

bil 9arabi ...

nouns change depending on whether they are singular or plural, if they are used with numbers, and if they are used with another noun:

tazkara *ticket,* **tazkartayn** *2 tickets,* **tazaakir** *3–10 tickets e.g.* **khams tazaakir** *5 tickets,* **tazkarat ruuHa** *a single ticket.*   **G1, G20**

2 **2•60** Mark Jones is booking train tickets at Aleppo station. Listen to the conversation and complete the travel information below. You'll hear **alaaf**, which is used to count thousands.

No. of tickets ....   Class ....

Type of ticket (single/return) ....   Destination ....

Day of travel ....   Total ticket price ....

3 **2•60** Listen again and write down which platform he needs to go to.

4 **2•61** Listen to four people buying train tickets at Casablanca station. Match the tickets with the prices as you hear them:

a a single to Rabat   b two return tickets to Al-Jadida

c three singles tickets to Fez d a single to the airport

12 dirhams   25 dirhams   45 dirhams   120 dirhams

Checking travel times

1   2•62 Listen to the key language:

ayy saa9a ...	What time ...
... il-qiTaar li Tanja?	... is the train to Tangiers?
... b-yimshi?	... does it leave? (m)
... b-yuSal marraaksh?	... does it arrive at Marrakesh? (m)
is-saa9a tamanya wa nuSS.	At 8.30. *Lit*. The time is eight thirty.
aymta il-qiTaar il-jaay?	When is the next train?
ba9d ...	In ...
... rub9 saa9a.	... a quarter of an hour.
... nuSS saa9a/saa9a.	... half an hour/an hour.

bil 9arabi ...

the hour is divided into: **nuSS** *a half,* **rub9** *a quarter*, **tult** *a third* (i.e. 20 minutes). Telling the time between the hours is done by either adding the word **wa** *plus* or **illa** *minus*: **9ashara wa nuSS** 10.30, **9ashara wa rub9** 10.15, **9ashara wa tult** 10.20. **9ashara illa rub9** 9.45, **9ashara illa tult** 9.40, **9ashara wa khamsa** 10.05, **9ashara illa 9ashara** 9.50.

25 past and 25 to the hour are calculated from the half hour: **talaata wa nuSS illa khamsa** 3.25 Lit. 3.30 *minus* 5. **arba9a wa nuSS wa khamsa** 4.35 Lit. 4.30 *and* 5.

2   2•63 Listen to a conversation at Rabat train station. You'll hear the word **ya9ni** meaning *I mean* or *you mean*.

a At what time does the next train to Tangiers leave?
b How much time does the passenger have before the train leaves?
c At what time does the train arrive at Tangiers?

3   2•64 Listen to people at Casablanca station checking train times and fill in the departure and arrival times:

	idh-dhahaab *departure*	**il-wuSuul** *arrival*
marraaksh *Marrakesh*		
Tanja *Tangiers*		
il-jadiida *Al-Jadida*		

4 How would you ask when the next train to Rabat is?

put it all together

1 Match the times with the clocks:

1 `02.25` 2 `10.30` 3 `08.35`

4 `04.45` 5 `06.10` 6 `11.55`

a is-saa9a 9ashara wa nuSS   b is-saa9a sitta wa 9ashara
c is-saa9a itnaashar illa   d is-saa9a itnayn wa nuSS
   khamsa   illa khamsa
e is-saa9a khamsa illa rub9   f is-saa9a tamanya wa
                                  nuSS wa khamsa

2 Say these times in Arabic:

a 7.30 b 12.45 c 2.15 d 3.25 e 4.20 f 9.50

3 Choose the correct verb from the box for each of the following questions:

1 aymta .... il-qiTaar min Tanja?
2 mumkin .... il-baaS?
3 ayy is-saa9a .... il-qiTaar il-jaay li Halab?
4 'addaysh .... ir-riHla min hawn li ba9albak?
5 laazim .... taksi, ya madaam.
6 mumkin .... bil qiTaar li dimaashq, ya sayyid?

> b-taakhud   tiruuH   b-yuSal
>
> b-yimshi   taakhdi   aakhud

4 Match the following words to form pairs.

a tazkarat   1 saa9aat
b maHaTTat   2 raqm itnayn
c daraja   3 il-jaay
d raSiif   4 il-qiTaar
e il-qiTaar   5 uula
f khams   6 ruuHa

1 **2•65** You are at the Abdalleh bus station in Amman and want to go to Damascus.

- Ask the woman at the ticket office if there's a bus to Damascus.
- ◆ **aywa, fiih baaS li dimashq kull yawm is-saa9a talaata.**
- Ask her how long the journey takes.
- ◆ **ir-riHla b-taakhud Hawaali arba9a saa9aat min 9ammaan li dimashq.**
- Ask her how much a ticket costs.
- ◆ **biddak tazkarat ruuHa aw ruuHa raj9a?**
- Tell her you'd like two single tickets, please.
- ◆ **Tayyib, haada khamsiin dinaar, min faDlak.**
- Say here you are.
- ◆ **shukran.**

2 **2•66** You are now in Damascus and would like to take the train to Aleppo.

- Ask the man in the ticket office when the next train leaves for Aleppo.
- ◆ **b-yimshi is-saa9a tamanya wa nuSS.**
- Find out what time the train arrives in Aleppo.
- ◆ **b-yuSal is-saa9a itnaa9sh wa nuSS.**
- Say you'd like a return ticket.
- ◆ **daraja taanya aw daraja uula?**
- Say first class, please. Ask how much it is.
- ◆ **tamanmiit lira.**
- Ask the price of second class.
- ◆ **sittmiyya wa khamsiin lira.**
- Say you would like one return ticket, first class, please.
- ◆ **itfaDDal. riHla sa9iida.** (*Bon Voyage*)
- Thank him, and ask which platform the train goes from.
- ◆ **raSiif raqm itnayn.**

quiz

1 Is **tis9a illa tult** 8.40, 9.20 or 9.40?
2 Which word means *journey/trip/flight*?
3 How do you say *second class return ticket*?
4 What's the difference between **is-saa9a arba9a** and **arba9a saa9aat**?
5 What does **il-jaay** mean?
6 Where are you most likely to see a **raSiif**?
7 How do you say *two tickets* in Arabic?
8 What's the difference between **laazim takkhud taksi** and **mumkin taakhud taksi**.

Now check whether you can ...

- say where you're going/you want to go
- ask if there are buses or trains
- find out when a bus/train leaves
- ask how long it takes to get to a place
- buy train tickets
- understand the time of day

You can use the internet to plan real or hypothetical journeys. You can practise what you've just learnt – work out what questions you'd need to ask to see if journeys are possible, and to find out prices and what time trains and buses leave and arrive. **riHla sa9iida!**

Modern Standard Arabic

The language used for writing and formal speech is known as Modern Standard Arabic (MSA). It is referred to in Arabic as **fuS-Ha** and is derived from Classical Arabic, the language of the Qur'an. You'll see MSA on signs and notices, in books, newspapers and magazines. MSA is not used in everyday interaction; although Arabic speakers might use it for formal discussions, they don't use it to speak to someone on an informal basis. As a visitor to the Arab world, the only time you're likely to hear it is if you watch the news on television or listen to announcements at stations and airports.

Spoken or colloquial Arabic **9amiyya** is the language used in everyday life. It varies from region to region but can be divided into five major dialects: Maghrebi (spoken in North Africa), Egyptian, Iraqi, Gulf and Levantine (spoken in Lebanon, Syria, Jordan and Palestine).

MSA and the regional dialects have many similarities. They tend to differ in the more everyday words and expressions. Below are some common differences:

What?

		What's your name?
Levantine	**shuu**	**shuu ismak/ismik?**
Gulf	**aysh**	**aysh ismak?**
Egyptian	**eeh**	**ismak eeh?**
MSA	**maa***	**maa ismuka/ismuki?**

* **maadha** before a verb: **maadha turiid?** *What would you like?* (to m)

The

		the house
Levantine and most spoken dialects	**il**	**il-bayt**
MSA	**al**	**al-bayt**

How much/how many?

	How much?	*How many?*
Levantine	**addaysh?**	**kam?**
Egyptian, Gulf	**bi kam?**	**kam?**
Moroccan	**bishHaal?**	**shHaal min?**
MSA	**bi kam?**	**kam?**

Want/would like

To say *want/would like*, Levantine Arabic uses: **biddi** *I want*, **biddak/biddik**
you (m/f) *want*, **biddu/biddha** *he/she wants*
and Egyptian: **9aawiz** *I/you* (m)/*he want(s)*, **9aawza** *I/you* (f)/*she want(s)*
MSA uses the verb **yuriidu**:

uriidu *I want/would like*   **yuriidu** *he wants/would like*

turiidu *you* (m) *want/would like*   **turiidu** *she wants/would like*

turiidiina *you* (f) *want/would like*

There is/there are

		there's a restaurant
Levantine, Egyptian and Gulf	**fiih**	**fiih maT9am**
Moroccan	**kayn**	**kayn maT9am**
MSA	**hunaaka**	**hunaaka maT9am**

Asking questions

Most Arabic spoken dialects including Levantine use intonation when
asking questions which require a yes or no answer, whereas MSA prefixes
the question with the word **hal**:
b-tHibb is-samak? → **hal tuHibb as-samak?** *Do you like fish?*

Not

In spoken Arabic, *not* is **mish** or **maa** (see G18 page 140):
ana mish min lubnaan. *I'm not from Lebanon.*
maa b-a9raf *I don't know.*

MSA has the verb **laysa** meaning *am/is/are not*:
lastu min lubnaan. *I'm not from Lebanon.*
lasta/lasti min al-urdun. *You* (m/f) *are not from Jordan.*
laysa/laysat mudarris/mudarrisa. *He's/she's not a teacher.*

Otherwise **laa** is used: **laa a9rif** *I don't know.*

In Egypt, North Africa and parts of the Levant, **-sh** is added to certain
negative structures:
maa fiih → **mafiish** *there isn't*
maa b-ashrab → **ma b-ashrabsh** *I don't drink*

il-akl laziiz!

understanding the menu

saying what you like and don't like

ordering a meal

expressing appreciation

Arabic food is really delicious and appeals to most people owing to its variety and sheer tastiness. One of the best-known aspects of Lebanese food is the **muqabbilaat** *starters* or **mazza** *mezze*, many of which are **nabaati** *vegetarian* and served with warm **khubz 9arabi** *pitta bread*.

Main courses are often **mashwiyyaat** *charcoal-grilled food,* such as **laHma** *meat*, **samak** *fish or* **dajaaj** *chicken,* which are popular throughout the Arab world. In Morocco the smell of the grilled meat and the aroma of the mint tea together is truly memorable. From vegetable couscous in the West to **betinjaan maHshi** *stuffed aubergines* in the East, there is always an alternative to meat. Although potatoes are eaten, rice is the staple food in the East whereas in North Africa it is couscous or bread.

For dessert many Arabs prefer a selection of **fawaakih** *fruit* after their meals. However the Arab world is famous for its **Hilu** *sweetmeats,* many of which contain honey, different types of nuts and filo pastry. There are also milk puddings flavoured with **ma' zaher** *rose water*.

Understanding the menu

1   **2•67** Look at **il-lista** *the menu* below. Listen to the waiter and tick the items he mentions from the menu. You'll hear **9andnaa** *we have.* What items aren't mentioned?

Lebanese salads and starters	السلطات اللبنانية والمقبلات	is-salaaTaat il-lubnaaniyya w-il muqabbilaat
smoked aubergine dip	متبل	mutabbal
beans	فول	fuul
falafel	فلافل	falaafil
crushed wheat & parsley salad	تبولة	tabbuuleh
charcoal grilled dishes	اطباق المشويات على الفحم	aTbaaq il-mashwiyyaat 9al-faHm
grilled lamb or beef	كفتة	kufta mashwiyya
grilled liver	كبدة	kibda mashwiyya
grilled chicken	دجاج	dajaaj mashwi
grilled fish	سمك	samak mashwi
mixed grill	مشوي مشكل	mashwi mishakkal
desserts	الحلو	il-Hilu
crème caramel	كريم كرامل	krim karamil
milk pudding	أم علي	umm 9ali
baklava	بقلاوة	ba'laawa
rice pudding	رز بحليب	ruzz bi Haliib
melted cheese covered with hot noodles	كنافة	kunaafa

2   **2•68** Farida is ready to order. Listen and make a note in English of the starters and main courses she asks for.

....

3   **2•69** After the main course, Hiba asks about dessert. What does she want? What does she order? Listen out for **9andkum**? *Do you have?* (plural)

Saying what you like and don't like

1   **2•70** Listen to the key language:

b-tHibb/b-tHibbi il-kibbeh?	Do you like meat rissoles? (to m/f)
b-aHibbu.	I like it. (m)
b-aHibbha.	I like it (f)/them.
b-aHibb is-samak.	I like fish.
maa b-aHibb il-falaafil.	I don't like falafel.
b-afaDDil id-dajaaj.	I prefer chicken.
b-taakul/b-taakli laHma?	Do you eat meat? (to m/f)
maa b-aakul laHma <u>abadan</u>.	I <u>never</u> eat meat.

---

bil 9arabi ...

The verb to like is **yiHibb**: **b-aHibb** *I like*, **b-tHibb** *you like* (m), **b-tHibbi** *you like* (f).

To make a general statement you use the definite article, e.g. **b-aHibb is-samak**. *I like fish*. Lit. *I like the fish*.

---

2   **2•71** Hasan Shoukry has invited Mark Jones out for dinner in Damascus. Listen and put a tick next to the foods Mark likes and a cross next to those he doesn't like.

falaafil   kibbeh   laHma   samak   ba'laawa   kunaafa

3   **2•72** Farida is checking what type of food her students David and Jacqueline like before ordering them lunch in Beirut. Listen and fill in the gaps. You'll hear **ya9ni** which means *so-so* in this context.

- ya Jacqueline, ... il-kufta il-mashwiyya?
- ya9ni, mish kitiir .... id-dajaaj.
- w-inta, ya David, ... il-kufta il-mashwiyya?
- laa', ana nabaati, maa b-aakul laHma .... !
- Tayyib, ... is-salaaTaat il-lubaaniyya?
- Tab9an, ... kitiir.

What do you think **nabaati** means?

4   Practise saying what foods you like using **b-aHibb**.

handwritten: karma ① hoada – lunch
② ashaa

Ordering a meal

1 2•73 Listen to the key language:

ayy naw9 ...	What kind of ...
... Hilu 9andkum?	... desserts do you have?
... akl nabaati 9andkum?	... vegetarian food do you have?
biddna Taawila li itnayn/arba9a.	We'd like a table for two/four.
il-akl hawn kwayyis kitiir.	The food here is very good.
haada kullu.	That's all.
mumkin kamaan khubz,	More bread, please. *Lit.* Is it
law samaHt/ samaHti?	possible more bread, please?

---

bil 9arabi ...

there are two ways of asking a question with *what*:
- **ayy** followed by a noun, indicating that there are options: **ayy naw9?** *What/which kind?* **ayy Hilu?** *What/which dessert?* **ayy lawn?** *What/which colour?*
- **shuu** followed by a noun or a verb: **shuu b-taakhud/b-taakhdi?** *What are you having?* **shuu ismak/ismik?** *What is your name?*

---

2 2•74 Ayman Shihadeh is ordering food for some conference delegates at the Abu Muusa grill in Irbid. Note how many of each dish he orders.

handwritten: market

dajaaj mashwi	2	mutabbal	4
kibda mashwiyya	1	SalSat TaHiina *sesame paste*	2
mashwi mishakkal	3	mujaddara *rice with lentils*	1

What else does he ask for?

3 2•75 Nadia Rif'at has invited her friend Khalid to her favourite restaurant in Amman. Listen to the conversation.

  a Why does Nadia like this restaurant so much?
  b Which two desserts are suggested by the waitress?
  c What is not available today?
  d What does Nadia say when asked **biddik shi taani**?

4 How would you say the following:
  • What type of **fawaakih** *fruit* have you got?
  • I'd like two mixed grills, please.
  • I'll have one aubergine dip and one rice with lentils.

Expressing appreciation

1 **2•76** Listen to the key language:

kiif <u>kaan</u> il-akl?	How <u>was</u> the food?
il-akl kaan laziiz.	The food was delicious.
khuSuuSan il-falaafil	especially the falafel
il-khidma kaanat mumtaaza fi9lan.	The service was <u>really</u> excellent.
il-garsawn kaan <u>laTiif</u> jiddan.	The waiter was very <u>nice</u>.
il-aanisa kaanat laTiifa jiddan.	The waitress was very nice.

---

bil 9arabi ...

there's no verb *to be* in the present tense: *I am in Beirut* is simply **ana fi bayruut**. Lit. *I in Beirut*. However, the verb *to be* exists in the past: **kunt** *I was*, **kaan** *he/it was*, **kunt/kunti** *you were* (m/f), **kaanat** *she/it was* and *they were* (f). **(ana) kunt fi bayruut**. *I was in Beirut.* **G15**

2 **2•77** Farida asks David and Jacqueline about their food. Listen and answer the following:

a Which dish did David like in particular?
b What impressed Jacqueline?
c What is Farida's final question to Jacqueline?

3 **2•78** Back at the Abu Muusa restaurant the manager asks if his guests have enjoyed the food. Listen and note down in Arabic the answers to his questions.

● **kiif kaan il-akl?**

◆ ....

◆ ....

● **wa kiif kaanat il-khidma?**

◆ ....

● **w-il garsawn?**

◆ ....

4 In Arabic how would you say:

● the food was delicious, especially the grilled chicken.

put it all together

1   Which of the following would you use:

1 id-dajaaj kaan laziiz fi9lan

2 b-aHibb il-mashwi il-mishakkal khuSuuSan

3 maa b-aHibb is-samak

4 b-aHibb il-laHma il-mashwiyya kitiir

5 b-afaDDil il-akl in-nabaati

6 maa b-aakul il-laHma abadan

a   if you don't eat meat at all?
b   to say you prefer vegetarian food?
c   to say you especially like the mixed grill?
d   to say you don't like fish?
e   to say that the chicken was really delicious?
f   to say you like grilled minced meat a lot?

2   For each question circle the correct answer.

a   b-tHibb is-samak? na9am, <u>b-aHibbu</u>/b-aHibbha kitiir.
b   b-taakul il-kufta? laa', maa <u>b-aaklu</u>/b-aakulha abadan.
c   b-tHibbi il-mujaddara? laa', maa b-aHibbu/<u>b-aHibbha</u>.
d   b-taakli ir-ruzz bi Haliib? na9am, b-aaklu/<u>b-aakulha</u>.
e   b-taakhud il-Hilu? na9am, <u>b-aakhdu</u>/b-aakhudha.
f   b-taakhud il-ba'laawa? na9am, b-aakhdu/<u>b-aakhudha</u>.

3   Number the following phrases in the order you might hear them in a restaurant:

a biddna Taawila li itnayn.   b haada kullu.
c marhaba, kam shakhS?   d itfaDDalu, ayy khidma?
e ayy naw9 mashwiyyaat   f biddna itnayn kufta
   9andkum?   mashwiyya, min faDlik.
g 9andna kufta   h biddak shi taani?
   mashwiyya, wa samak
   mashwi, wa dajaaj
   mashwi il-yawm.

now you're **talking!**

1 **2•79** Imagine you're in a restaurant on the Syrian coast with your friend who is a vegetarian. Ask the waiter for a table for two.

- **itfaDDalu.**
- ◆ Ask the waiter what type of vegetarian food he has.
- **9andnaa salaaTaat kitiir Tab9an.**
- ◆ Say OK and ask for one aubergine dip and one crushed wheat and parsley salad.
- **wa biddak mashwiyyaat?**
- ◆ Say you'll have one mixed grill.
- **HaDirtak biddak shi taani?**
- ◆ Say yes, you'd like more bread.
- **HaaDir, ya ustaaz.**

2 **2•80** You've just finished eating at a restaurant in Homs and the manager comes over to ask you how you found the food. You'll hear **in-shaa' allaah** which means *God willing*.

- **ahlan wa sahlan, ana mudiir il-maT9am. kiif kaan il-akl?**
- ◆ Say that the food was really delicious.
- **kiif kaanat il-muqabbilaat?**
- ◆ Say the starters were delicious as well, especially the beans.
- **wa kiif kaanat il-khidma?**
- ◆ Say the service was excellent, and the waiter was very nice.
- **shukran kitiir. marra taanya in-shaa' allaah?**
- ◆ Say yes, God willing.

quiz

1 Would **mujaddara** be suitable for a vegetarian?

2 At a restaurant, how would you say *We'd like a table for three*?

3 Which of the following is the odd one out and why? **kunaafa, mutabbal, tabbuuleh, falaafil, fuul.**

4 What does **kamaan khubz** mean?

5 Which adjective would you use to complete this phrase: **il-khidma kaanat** ...... **laziiza/mumtaaza.**

6 How do you say *I never drink beer*?

7 How would you ask someone how the food was?

8 If **akalt** means *I/you* (m) *ate*, how would you ask *What did you eat yesterday*?

Now check whether you can ...

- understand the Arabic for basic menu items
- ask for a table in a restaurant
- ask what kind of food is available in a restaurant
- order a meal
- say what you like, don't like and prefer
- pay a compliment on the food and service

Now get ready for the final Checkpoint, which covers the whole of **Talk Arabic**, with a bit of revision. Listen to the conversations again, test your knowledge of the key language by covering up the English and Arabic in turn, and use the quizzes and checklists at the end of each unit to assess how much you remember.

Checkpoint 3

You're on a tour of the Middle East and you've just arrived in Amman where you're meeting up with your friend, Khalid.

1   You have a booking at the Shepheard's Hotel in Amman for five nights. At reception which of the following would be the correct thing to say:

    a   ahlan wa sahlan. Hajazt ghurfa hawn.
    b   is-salaam 9alaykum. biddi ghurfa li khams layaali.
    c   is-salaam 9alaykum. 9andi Hajz li khams layaali.
    d   ahlan wa sahlan. 9andak ghurfa li khams layaali?
    e   is-salaam 9alaykum. Hajazt khams ghuraf hawn.

2   **2•81** Listen to the receptionist and make a note of the things she says to you:

    1   ....
    2   ....
    3   ....
    4   ....
    5   ....

3   **2•82** You visit Khalid in his office. Listen to him telling Nadia his travel plans for the week and note down what he's doing including when he'll be in Baalbek, Damascus, Beirut and London. Listen out for **abi** *my father* and **ummi** *my mother*.

Mon		**Fri**	
....		....	
Tues		**Sat**	
....		....	
Wed		**Sun**	
....		....	
Thur			
....			

4   **2.83** Listen to the following information, and write down where you are likely to be in each situation:

1   2   ....

3   4   ....

5   6   ....

7   8   ....

5   You go with Khalid to Damascus and while he's working you get ready to explore. How would you ask the receptionist:

a   if you can use the internet?
b   how to get to the Umayyad Mosque?
c   where you can buy an English newspaper?
d   if the National Museum is far from the hotel?

The receptionist gives you these directions to the Mosque: **ruuH 9ala Tuul, wa fi aakhir ish-shaari9 liff yamiin. khud taani yasaar. il-jaami9 il-umawi mi'aabil is-suu'**. Write them down in English.

....

....

....

6   After your visit to the Umayyad Mosque you go to a café in the Old City and get talking to a young man called Bilal sitting at the next table. What questions do you need to ask him to get these replies?

a   ....
   ● **b-atkallam ingliizi shwayya.**

b   ....
   ● **ana Taalib fi jaami9at dimashq.**

c   ....
   ● **laa', ana mish min dimashq, ana min Homs.**

d   ....
   ● **ana mish mitzawwij.**

e   ....
   ● **9andi itnayn wa 9ishriin sana.**

f   ....
   ● **laa', ana maa b-aHibb il-akl il-ingliizi.**

7 You offer Bilal a drink as he has given you some good advice for your trip tomorrow to Aleppo.

- Ask him what he would like to drink.
- ◆ **b-aakhud 9aSiir rumaan**.
- Ask the waitress for a mint tea for you and Bilal's juice.
- ◆ **itfaDDalu**.
- Ask for the bill.
- ◆ **miyya wa sittiin lira, min faDlak**.

How much change would you get from 200 Syrian pounds?

8 You're now at Damascus station trying to buy a second class return ticket to Aleppo. You need to find out what time the train leaves, and how long it takes. For each question choose the correct options.

a **law samaHt, ayy saa9a b-yimshi/b-yuSal il-qiTaar il-jaay li Halab?**

b **'addaysh b-taakhud/b-tiruuH ir-riHla min hawn li Halab?**

c **biddi tazkarat ruuHa raj9a/ruuHa, daraja uula/daraja taanya, min faDlak.**

9 In Aleppo you visit its famous covered market where one of the vendors asks you if you would like to buy something from his stall.

Say the following to him:
- No thanks, I just want to look.
- Yes, the dish is pretty, but I have a lot of dishes.
- Can I have a look at the coffee pot?
- How much is it?
- No, that's very expensive. No way!
- How about 200 Syrian pounds?
- I'm sorry, that's a lot!

10 You've arranged to meet Bilal and some of his friends that evening for dinner. Tareq is from Beirut and is an accountant in Damascus, Sophie Lowry is a teacher from Edinburgh.

How would they answer these questions:
- **shuu ismak/ismik?**
- **min wayn inta/inti?**
- **shuu shughlak/shughlik?**

11 You're going to order for everyone, so make a note on the menu of who wants what:

Sophie would like: smoked aubergine dip, falafel, grilled fish, milk pudding.

Tareq would like: beans, mixed grill, baklava.

Bilal would like: rice with lentils, grilled lamb, rice pudding.

You would like: crushed wheat and parsley salad, grilled chicken, crème caramel.

How would you ask a waitress for sesame paste and more bread?

12 After an excellent visit to Damascus you get a taxi to the airport to fly back to London. Fill in the gaps in the conversation you have with the driver. **9al wa't** means *on time*.

- **mumkin .... lil-maTaar, law samaHt?**
- **itfaDDal.**
- **'addaysh .... min hawn lil-maTaar?**
- **ta'riiban .... waaHda. wayn raayiH HaDirtak?**
- **ana .... li London.**
- **kiif kaanat dimashq?**
- **.................. mumtaaza. dimashq madiina ....**
- **aymta ....**
- **.................. saa9atayn.**
- **in-shaa' allaah b-nuSal il-maTaar 9al-wa't!**
- **..................**

السلطات اللبنانية والمقبلات	is-salaaTaat il-lubnaaniyya w-il muqabbilaat
متبل	mutabbal
فول	fuul
فلافل	falaafil
تبولة	tabbuuleh
مجدرة	mujaddara

اطباق المشويات على الفحم	aTbaaq il-mashwiyyaat 9al-faHm
كفتة	kufta mashwiyya
كبدة	kibda mashwiyya
دجاج	dajaaj mashwi
سمك	samak mashwi
مشوى	mashwi
مشكل	mishakkal

الحلو	il-Hilu
كريم كرامل	krim karamil
أم علي	umm 9ali
بقلاوة	ba'laawa
رز بحليب	ruzz bi Haliib
كنافة	kunaafa

in-shaa' allaah
b-yaakhud
saa9a
jamiila
taakhudni
ir-riHla
raayiH
ba9d
kaanat

mabruuk! *Congratulations!* You have now reached the end of **Talk Arabic**. **bit-tawfii' fil musta'bal** *We wish you success in the future.*

transcripts and answers

This section contains the scripts of all the **Talk Arabic** conversations. Answers which consist of words/ phrases from the conversations are in bold type; other answers are given separately.

Unit 1

Page 8

2 • **is-salaam 9alaykum.**
  ◆ wa 9alaykum is-salaam.
  • **kiif il-Haal?**
  ◆ bi-khayr il-Hamdullilaah.
  • **ahlan.**
  ◆ ahlan. kiif il-Haal?
  • il-Hamdullilaah.

3 • **ahlan wa sahlan,** ya madaam Fawziyya.
  ◆ **ahlan fiik. kiif il-Haal?**
  • **bi-khayr, shukran. w-inti?**
  ◆ **il-Hamdullilaah.**

4 • **ahlan, ya Mona.** kiif il-Haal?
  ◆ **bi-khayr, shukran. w-inta?**
  • il-Hamdullilaah.

Page 9

2 • **SabaaH il-khayr, madaam Fawziyya.**
  ◆ SabaaH in-nuur.

  • **masaa il-khayr, aanisa Hoda.**
  ◆ ahlan, masaa in-nuur. kiif il-Haal?
  • bi-khayr, il-Hamdullilaah, w-inti?
  ◆ il-Hamdullilaah, bi-khayr, shukran.

  • **SabaaH il-khayr, sayyid Hamdi.**
  ◆ SabaaH in-nuur.

  • **ma9a as-salaama, sayyid Haddad.**
  ◆ allaah yisalmik.

3 • allaah yisalmak.
  • ma9a as-salaama. ashuufak ba9dayn.
  • allaah yisalmik.
  • SabaaH il-khayr, kiif Haalak?
  • ma9a as-salaama, ashuufik ba9dayn.
1 m; 2 m; 3 f; 4 m; 5 f

4 SabaaH il-khayr, ya Rania. allaah yisalmak. ashuufik ba9dayn.

Page 10

2 • law samaHt, HaDirtak Lutfi?
  ◆ laa', ana mish Lutfi, ana Jamal.
  • law samaHti, HaDirtik Zeinab?
  ◆ aywa, ana Zeinab.
  • ahlan wa sahlan, ya Zeinab.
  ◆ ahlan fiiki.
  • HaDirtak Nureddine?
  ◆ laa', ana mish Nureddine, ana Mustafa!
  • wa HaDirtik Samia?
  ◆ laa', ana mish Samia, ana Nadia!
She's looking for Lufti, Zeinab, Nureddine, Samia.

3 • **law samaHt,** HaDirtak Mustafa Amin?
  ◆ **aywa,** ana Mustafa Amin, wa **HaDirtak?**
  • ana Adnan Hasan.
  ◆ ahlan wa sahlan. **ana** Mustafa Amin. **HaDirtik** Dalia Mustafa?
  • laa', **ana mish** Dalia Mustafa. ana Amira Ahmad.
  ◆ ahlan, ya Amira!

Page 11

2 • ahlan wa sahlan, **ismi** Sami Suleiman, **shuu ismik?**
  ◆ **ahlan fiik. ismi** Nadia Rif'at.
  • **tasharrafna.**
  ◆ **ish-sharaf ili.**
shuu ismak is left over

3 • ahlan wa sahlan, **shuu ismik?**

- **ismi** Zeinab, **w-inta**?
- ismi Ahmad, **tasharrafna**. **shuu ismak**?
- ismi Farid.
- marHaba.
- marHabtayn.

4 • ahlan wa sahlan, ismi Omar. shuu ismak?
- ahlan fiik, ismi Sami.
- marHaba Sami.
- marHabtayn. shuu ismik?
- ismi Tara, tasharrafna.
- ish-sharaf ili. w-inta, shuu ismak?
- ismi Abdu, kiif il-Haal?
- bi-khayr, il-Hamdullilaah.
  1 c; 2 a; 3 d; 4 b

Page 12

1 *a* 7; *b* 1; *c* 8; *d* 5; *e* 9; *f* 3; *g* 6; *h* 2; *i* 4

2 *a* SabaaH il-khayr/SabaaH in-nuur; *b* masaa il-khayr/masaa in-nuur; *c* is-salaam 9alaykum/wa 9alaykum is-salaam; *d* ma9a as-salaama/ allaah yisalmik/yisalmak.

3 *a* ahlan, ya Ahmad; *b* ahlan fiik; *c* w-inti, kiif il-Haal?

Page 13

1 • masaa il-khayr.
- **masaa in-nuur.**
- ahlan wa sahlan, ismi Nabiil. shuu ismik?
- **ahlan fiik, ismi Barbara**.
- tasharrafna.
- **ish-sharaf ili.**

2 • **tasharrafna. kiif il-Haal?**
- bi-khayr, shukran. il-Hamdullilaah. wa HaDirtik?
- **bi-khayr, shukran.**
- ma9a as-salaama. ashuufik ba9dayn.
- **allaah yisalmik.**

3 • **ahlan wa sahlan.**
- ahlan fiiki, ya Barbara.
- **ahlan, inta Mustafa?**
- laa', ana mish Mustafa, ismi Mourad!

1 in reply to is-salaam 9alaykum; *2* HaDirtik; *3 excuse me to a man, excuse me to a woman; 4 morning; 5* ahlan wa sahlan, marHaba, is-salaam 9alaykum; *6* shuu ismak? *7* ish-sharaf ili; *8* ashuufak bukra.

Unit 2
Page 18

2 • ahlan, min wayn inta, ya George?
- ana min **lubnaan**.
- inta min il-maghrib, ya Muhsin?
- laa', ana mish min il-maghrib. ana min **maSr**.
- w-inta, ya Tareq?
- ana min **is-sa9uudiyya**.
- min wayn inti, ya Nadia? inti min is-sa9uudiyya kamaan?
- laa', ana min **il-urdun**.
- wa HaDirtik?
- ana ismi Ruba, ana min **suuriya**!

George: Lebanon; Muhsin: Egypt; Tareq: Saudi Arabia; Nadia: Jordan; Ruba: Syria

3 • ahlan wa sahlan. ismi Hasan Shoukry.
- ahlan fiik, ismi Mark Jones. ana min London. min wayn inta, ya Hasan?
- ana min maSr.
- inta min il-qaahira?
- laa', ana min **iskandariyya**.

4 min wayn inti, ya Farida?

Page 19

2 amriika, amriiki, amriikiyya; iskutlanda, iskutlandi, iskutlandiyya; fransa, fransi, fransiyya; ingilterra, ingliizi, ingliiziyya; irlanda, irlandi, irlandiyya; maSr, maSri, maSriyya; il-maghrib, maghribi, maghribiyya; is-sa9uudiyya, sa9uudi, sa9uudiyya; tuunis,

tuunisi, tuunisiyya; suuriya, suuri, suuriyya

3 • Hussein, min wayn inta?
  ◆ ana **lubnaani**.
  • Maha, inti lubnaaniyya kamaan?
  ◆ laa', ana mish lubnaaniyya, ana **maghribiyya**.
  • Adam, inta amriiki?
  ◆ aywa, ana **amriiki**.
  • Jacqueline, inti min fransa – inti fransiyya?
  ◆ aywa, ana **fransiyya**.
  • David, inta min briiTaanya?
  ◆ aywa, min briiTaanya, ana **iskutlandi**.
Hussein: Lebanese; Maha: Moroccan; Adam: American; Jacqueline: French; David: Scottish.

Page 20

2 • wayn **saakna** fil-urdun, ya Nadia?
  ◆ ana saakna **fi** 9ammaan.
  • w-inta ya Muhsin, **wayn** saakin?
  ◆ ana saakin **fil-qaahira**.
  • inta **saakin** fil-qaahira kamaan, ya George?
  ◆ laa', ana **mish saakin** fil-qaahira, ana saakin fi bayruut.

3 sayyid Adnan min suuriyya, bass huwwa saakin fi baghdaad. madaam Amira saakna fid-daar il-bayDa. sayyid Hussein min maSr, bass saakin fi Taraablus. sayyid Mustafa saakin fi jadda. madaam Lucy saakna fil-jazaa'ir, bass hiyya briiTaaniyya.
1 e; 2 a; 3 c; 4 d; 5 b

Page 21

2 6, 9, 1, 3, 5, 8, 0, 2, 10, 4, 7

4 • raqm tilifawn il-maktab 0134 0460
    wa raqm tilifawn il-bayt 0146 0179
    wa raqm il-mubayl 0993 2271.
office: 0134 0460; home: 0146 0179; mobile: 0993 2271

5 • shuu raqm tilifawn il-maktab?
  ◆ **raqm tilifawn il-maktab Sifr, waaHid, arba9a, arba9a, itnayn, sab9a, sab9a, sitta.**
  • 9andik mubayl?
  ◆ **aywa, raqm il-mubayl Sifr, tis9a, tis9a, arba9a, sab9a, sab9a, tis9a, itnayn. wa raqm tilifawn il-bayt Sifr, waaHid, arba9a, arba9a, waaHid, sitta, sitta, khamsa.**
  • Tayyib. shukran.
office: 0144 2776; mobile: 0994 7792; home: 0144 1665

Page 22

1 *a* ana min maSr, saakin fil-qaahira. ana maSri.
  b ana min il-maghrib, saakna fid-daar il-bayDa. ana maghribiyya.
  c ana min is-sa9uudiyya, saakin fi jadda. ana sa9uudi.
  d ana min suuriya, saakna fi dimashq. ana suuriyya.
  e ana min iskutlanda, saakin fi Edinburgh. ana iskutlandi.

2 *a* tis9a, 9; *b* tamanya, 8; *c* arba9a, 4; *d* khamsa, 5

3 Lucy Abbott; ingilterra; ingliiziyya

4 il-maghrib: sitta; fransa: itnayn; tuunis: talaata: lubnaan: waaHid; iskutlanda: khamsa: suuriya: tis9a; maSr: arba9a; il-urdun: sab9a

Page 23

1 • min wayn inta?
  ◆ **ana min fransa. inta min il-urdun?**
  • laa', ana min tuunis. wayn saakin?
  ◆ **saakin fi Paris. shuu ismak?**
  • ismi Jamal, marHaba.

2 • inti min fransa kamaan?
  ◆ **laa', ana min briiTaanya**.
  • wayn saakna?
  ◆ **saakna fi York**.
  • shuu ismik?
  ◆ **ismi Louise**.

3 • raqm tilifawn il-bayt: Sifr, waaHid, tis9a, sitta, sitta, khamsa, tamanya
Jamal's home number is: 019 6658.

• **raqm il-mubayl: Sifr, tis9a, sab9a, waaHid, arba9a, arba9a, khamsa, talaata, sab9a, sitta.**

Page 24

1 Saudi Arabia; 2 maghribi means Moroccan, the other two are countries; 3 ana min ingilterra, saakin (m)/saakna (f) fi London; 4 tamanya, 9ashara; 5 ana maSriyya; 6 huwwa min suuriya; 7 a woman; 8 shuu raqm tilifawn il-maktab?

Unit 3

Page 28

2 • haada jawzi, Sinaan.
  • ahlan wa sahlan, ismi Ewan.
  • ahlan fiik.
  • wa haadi zamiilti Shahla.
  • marHaba.
  • marHabtayn, ana Ewan.
Sinaan is Farida's husband, Shahla is Farida's colleague.

3 • haadi **marti** Layla.
  • ahlan wa sahlan.
  • ahlan fiik.
  • wa haada **SaaHibi** Adnaan.
  • marHaba, ya Adnaan.
  • marHabtayn.
  • wa **haadi SaaHibti** Marwa.
  • tasharrafna.
Marwa is Shahla's friend.

4 *a haadi marti Suzanne; b haada jawzi John; c haada zamiili Lutfi; d haadi SaaHibti Jamila.*

Page 29

2 • inta mitzawwij, ya Nabiil?
  • aywa, ana mitzawwij wa marti min amriika.
  • 9andak awlaad?

• aywa, 9andi arba9a awlaad, ibn waaHid wa talaat banaat.
• w-inti, ya Hasna, inti mitzawwija?
• aywa, ana mitzawwija wa 9andi bint waaHda. w-inta, ya Mark?
• ana mish mitzawwij, wa maa 9andi awlaad.
Nabiil Shukri: married; Hasna Sabri: married; Mark Jones: not married.

3 *Nabiil Shukri: 1 son, 3 daughters; Hasna Sabri: 1 daughter; Mark Jones: no children.*

4 • inti mitzawwija, ya Samia?
  • aywa, ana mitzawwija.
  • 9andik awlaad?
  • 9andi talaat banaat. w-inti, ya Linda?
  • **ana mish mitzawwija, wa maa 9andi awlaad.**

Page 30

2 • inta muhandis, ya Ewan?
  • laa', ana mish muhandis, ana **Taalib** fil-jaami9a.
  • inti Taaliba kamaan, ya Brigitte?
  • laa', ana mish Taaliba, ana **mumarriDa**.
  • w-inta, ya John?
  • ana **muHaasib**.
  • ya Hilary, shuu shughlik?
  • ana **Tabiiba**.
a 3; b 4; c 1; d 2

3 • Ahmad Khaalid muHaasib fi maktab fi 9ammaan.
  • Leila Muraad ustaaza fi jaami9at baghdaad.
  • Mahmuud Saber Tabiib fi mustashfa fi Liverpool.
  • Jumaana Dalaal mudarrisa fi madrasa fi iskandariyya, wa Salah Nazmi muhandis fi sharika amriikiyya.
Ahmad Khaalid: accountant in an office in Amman; Leila Muraad: lecturer at Baghdad university; Mahmuud Saber: doctor in hospital in Liverpool; Jumaana Dalaal: teacher in a school in

Alexandria; Salah Nazmi: engineer in an American company.

4 shuu shughlak, ya Mark?

Page 31

2 17, 11, 20, 12, 16, 15, 19

4 ● ya Mark, haada Muhammed.
  ◆ ahlan, ya Muhammed. 9andak kam sana?
  ● 9andi **tamanta9shar sana.**
  ◆ wa haada Hasan, wa haada George.
  ● ahlan wa sahlan, ismi Mark. 9andak kam sana, ya Hasan?
  ◆ 9andi **talata9shar sana.**
  ◆ w-inta, ya George?
  ◆ 9andi **arba9tashar sana.**
Muhammed 18; Hasan 13; George 14

5 ● 9andik awlaad, ya Shahla?
  ◆ 9andi walad wa bint.
  ● il-walad shuu ismu?
  ◆ ismu Sinaan wa 9andu Hida9shar sana.
  ● wa shuu ism bintik?
  ◆ binti ismha Latifa.
  ● wa kam sana 9andha?
  ◆ 9andha khamasta9shar sana.
Latifa is older.

Page 32

1 *a* 3; *b* 4; *c* 6; *d* 5; *e* 1; *f* 2

2 *a* mitzawwij; *b* arba9a awlaad; *c* arba9a siniin; *d* 9ashar siniin; *e* sab9ata9shar sana

3 haadi marti, Saida. hiyya mudarrisa. haada SaaHibi, Ashraf. huwwa mitzawwij. huwwa muHaasib. haadi zamiilti Lina. hiyya mish mitzawwija. hiyya Tabiiba.

Page 33

1 ● ahlan. min wayn inta?
  ◆ **min Manchester fi ingilterra.**
  ● shuu ismak?
  ◆ **ismi David.**
  ● haadi martak?

◆ **aywa, ismha Rachel.**
● shuu shuglak?
◆ **ana mudarris.**
● wa 9andak awlaad?
◆ **aywa, 9andi bint waaHda, ismha Alison.**
● kam sana 9andha?
◆ **9andha itna9ashar sana.**

2 ● **HaDirtak mitzawwij?**
  ◆ aywa, ana mitzawwij.
  ● **haadi martak?**
  ◆ aywa, ismha Hiba.
  ● **9andak awlaad?**
  ◆ 9andi ibn waaHid.
  ● **shuu ismu?**
  ◆ ismu Hussein.
  ● **kam sana 9andu?**
  ◆ 9andu tis9ata9shar sana.
  ● **huwwa fil-madrasa?**
  ◆ laa', huwwa Taalib fi jaami9at dimashq.

Page 34

1 *a hospital;* 2 bint waaHda wa ibn waaHid; 3 sitta; 4 sana; 5 *female student;* 6 haadi SaaHibti, Rana; 7 *woman;* 8 ana mish mitzawwija; 9 maa 9andi mubayl.

Unit 4

Page 38

2 ● shuu b-tHibbi?
  ◆ biddi waaHid shaay bi Haliib. wa itnayn shaay biduun Haliib, wa talaata 'ahwa maZbuuT, wa waaHid 'ahwa biduun sukkar, min faDlak.
a 1; b 2; c 3; d 1

3 ● **shuu** b-tHibbi?
  ◆ min faDlak. biddi waaHid **'ahwa** wa waaHid **shaay.**
  ● **bi** sukkar aw **biduun** sukkar?
  ◆ shaay biduun sukkar, wa 'ahwa **maZbuuT.**
  ● HaaDir.

Page 39

2 ● ayy khidma?

- ayy 9aSiir 9andak?
- fiih 9aSiir burtu'aan, wa 9aSiir manga, wa 9aSiir shammaam.
- biddi waaHid **9aSiir burtu'aan** wa itnayn **9aSiir shammaam**.
- HaaDir.
- aah…wa **'aniinat mayya ma9daniyya,** min faDlak.
- HaaDir.
- law samaHt, 9andak biira?
- laa', maa fiih biira.

Orange juice, melon juice, mineral water. He asks if they have beer.

3
- marHaba.
- marHabtayn. 9andak 9aSiir tuffaaH?
- laa', maa 9andi. fiih 9aSiir manga wa 9aSiir lamuun.
- Tayyib, biddi waaHid 'ahwa, min faDlak, wa 9ilbat cola.
- HaaDir.

She orders coffee and cola; because they don't have any.

4 law samaHti, biddi waaHid shaay bi Haliib, wa itnayn 'ahwa maZbuuT, wa waaHid 9aSiir tuffaaH, wa itnayn 9aSiir shammaam, wa waaHid 'aniinat mayya ma9daniyya, wa talaata biira, min faDlik.

2
- b-tishrabi shaay, ya Nadia?
- laa' shukran, maa biddi shaay. **b-ashrab 'ahwa**, min faDlak.
- Tayyib. 9ashaanak ya Hasan, b-tHibb shaay aw 'ahwa?
- waaHid **shaay biduun sukkar** 9ashaani, min faDlak.
- HaaDir.

Nadia: coffee; Hasan: tea without sugar.

3
- ahlan, ya Nabiil! kiif il-haal?
- bi-khayr shukran. w-inta?
- il-hamdullilaah. shuu b-tishrab?
- ana b-aakhud 'ahwa bi Haliib, min faDlak.
- biddak 'aniinat mayya kamaan?

- laa' shukran, maa biddi mayya, w-inta?
- 9ashaani … b-aakhud 'ahwa bass.

2 9ishriin, talatiin, talaata wa talatiin, arba9iin, arba9a wa arba9iin, khamsiin, khamsa wa sittiin, tamanya wa saba9iin.
22 not mentioned.

3 sitta wa 9ishriin, talaata wa khamsiin, waaHid wa sittiin, arba9a wa saba9iin, sab9a wa saba9iin, waaHid wa tamaniin, tis9a wa tis9iin, miyya.

5
- il-Hisaab, min faDlak.
- Tayyib … il-'ahwa bi arba9iin lira, wa il-9aSiir bi khamsa wa talatiin lira. il-majmuu9 khamsa wa sab9iin lira, min faDlak.
- itfaDDal, shukran kitiir.
- 9afwan!

The coffee is 40 Syrian pounds, the juice is 35 Syrian pounds, total is 75 Syrian pounds.

6
- il-Hisaab, min faDlak.
- sitta wa talatiin lira, min faDlik.
- itfaDDal arba9iin … wa khalli il-baa'i 9ashaanak.
- shukran kitiir.

The tip is 4 Syrian pounds.

1 *a* 5; *b* 1; *c* 2; *d* 4; *e* 3.

2 *1* talaata wa tis9iin; *2* tamanya wa saba9iin; *3* tis9a wa tamaniin; *4* itnayn wa talatiin; *5* talaata wa khamsiin; *6* arb9a wa 9ishriin.

3 *a one tea with sugar; b three orange juices; c two semi-sweet coffees; d lemon juice; e coffee and a bottle of mineral water.*

1
- ayy khidma?
- **biddi itnayn 'ahwa maZbuuT wa waaHid shaay, min faDlak.**

- bi Haliib aw biduun Haliib?
- **bi Haliib.**
- HaaDir.

2 ● **il-Hisaab, min faDlak.**
  - itfaDDali, saba9iin lira.
  - **itfaDDal, tamaniin lira. khalli il-baa'i 9ashaanak.**
  - shukran kitiir. ma9a as-salaama.
  - **allaah yisalmak.**

3 ● ahlan. shuu b-tishrabi?
  - **ahlan fiik. 9andak biira?**
  - laa', maa fiih biira. 9andi 9aSiir burtu'aan aw 9aSiir tuffaaH.
  - **b-aakhud 9aSiir burtu'aan, min faDlak.**
  - itfaDDali.

Page 44

1 9afwan; 2 bass; 3 88; 4 9andik 9aSiir rumaan? 5 min faDlak; 6 9ashaani; 7 biduun sukkar; 8 the bill.

Checkpoint 1

Pages 45–48

1 *a* ahlan wa sahlan; *b* ana bi-khayr, shukran; *c* tasharrafna; *d* 9andak kam sana?; *e* SabaaH il-khayr; *f* haadi marti; *g* wayn saakna?; *h* ana mish mitzawwij(a).

2 *a* SabaaH (the others are all drinks); *b* mubayl (the others are all professions); *c* mitzawwij (the others are all places); *d* tuunisiyya (others are male nationalities); *e* ukht (others are male relatives); *f* 9ilba (others are fruit); *g* sharika (others are people); *h* Tayyib (the others are all greetings)

3 *a* shuu ismak?; *b* 9andak kam sana?; *c* min wayn inta?; *d* wayn saakin?; *e* shuu shuglak?; *f* inta mitzawwij?; *g* 9andi awlaad?

4 ● is-salaam 9alaykum, ana ismi Ahmad. ana maSri min il-qaahira.
  - wa 9alaykum is-salaam. ismi Lutfi. ana suuri min dimashq.
- wa ana Naima. ana maghribiyya min ir-ribaaT.
  - ahlan ya Naima, ismi Suhail. ana sa9uudi min ir-riyaaD.
- wa ismi Nadia. ana lubnaaniyya min bayruut.
  - ahlan fiiki. ismi Susan. ana ingliiziyya min Leeds.

Ahmad: maSri; *Lutfi:* suuri; *Naima:* maghribiyya; *Suhail:* sa9uudi; *Nadia:* lubnaaniyya; *Susan:* ingliiziyya

5 ● liibya - itnayn waaHid tamanya.
  - il-maghrib - itnayn waaHid itnayn.
- maSr - itnayn Sifr.
  - il-imaaraat - tis9a sab9a waaHid.
- lubnaan - tis9a sitta waaHid.
  - suuriya - tis9a sitta talaata.
- il-urdun - tis9a sitta itnayn.
  - is-sa9uudiyya - tis9a sitta sitta.

1 218; 2 212; 3 20; 4 971; 5 961; 6 963; 7 962; 8 966

6 *a* ayy 9aSiir 9andak/ik?; *b* shuu b-tHibb/i?; shuu b-tishrab/i?; *c* bi Haliib aw biddun Haliib?; *d* fiih/9andak/ik 9aSiir lamuun? *e* 9ashaanak/ik?

7 *1 d; 2 i; 3 g; 4 j; 5 h; 6 a; 7 e; 8 c; 9 f; 10 b*

8 ● marHaba.
  - marHabtayn.
- ana ismi Lutfi. shuu ism HaDirtik?
  - ismi Mona.
- ahlan wa sahlan, ya Mona. min wayn inti?
  - ana min ir-ribaaT fil-maghrib, bass saakna fi London.
- ana marti maghribiyya. ana min il-urdun. HaDirtik mitzawwija?
  - laa', ana mish mitzawwija, bass 9andi SaaHib min ingilterra. 9andak awlaad?
- 9andi ibn waaHid, ismu Hasan.
  - wa kam sana 9andu?
- khams siniin. wa shuu shughlik, ya Mona?

- ana Tabiiba fi mustashfa.
- ana Tabiib kamaan!

Doctor, London, Jordanian, married, boyfriend, one son.

9 *a* khamsa wa khamsiin lira; *b* tis9a wa saba9iin lira; *c* arba9a wa tis9iin lira; *d* sitta wa tamaniin lira.

10 *a* biddi itnayn shaay; *b* 9ashaani waaHid 'ahwa; *c* b-aakhud talaata mayya; *d* biddi arb9a 9aSiir burtu'aan; *e* 9ashaani waaHid cola; *f* b-aakhud itnayn 9aSiir shammaam; *g* biddi khamsa 'ahwa bi Haliib; *h* b-aakhud waaHid shaay bi na9na9.

Unit 5

Page 50

2 suu'; maktab bariid; dukkaan; dakaakiin; bank; ba'aal; maqha internet; matHaf; suubermarket; fundu'; maHaTTa; jaami9

3 • fiih **maktab bariid** hawn, wa fiih **suu**', wa fiih **bank**, wa fiih **dakaakiin kitiir**.

1 post office; 2 market; 3 bank; 4 many shops

4 • law samaHti, mumkin ti'uuli li fiih maqha internet hawn?
- aywa, fiih maqha internet.
- wa fiih suubermarket?
- aywa, fiih.
- fiih ba'aal hawn?
- laa', maa fiih.
- law samaHti, mumkin ti'uuli li fiih matHaf hawn?
- aywa, fiih matHaf.

internet café ✓; supermarket ✓; grocer's ✗; museum ✓

Page 51

2 • SabaaH il-khayr.
- SabaaH in-nuur.
- mumkin ti'uuli li wayn maktab il-bariid?
- maktab il-bariid mi'aabil il-fundu'.
- wa mumkin ti'uuli li wayn

is-suu'?
- is-suu' fi wasT il-madiina.
- wa maqha il-internet?
- maqha il-internet janb il-madrasa.
- wa fiih maHaTTa hawn?
- aywa, fiih maHaTTa waraa il-jaami9.

A station; B post office; C internet café; D market.

3 • law samaHt, fiih matHaf hawn?
- aywa, fiih matHaf.
- mumkin ti'uul li wayn il-matHaf biZ-ZabT?
- il-matHaf ba9d il-jaami9, mi'aabil il-maHaTTa.
- shukran kitiir.

The museum is past the mosque and opposite the station.

4 mumkin ti'uli li wayn il-matHaf biZ-ZabT?

Page 52

2 yawm il-aHad, yawm il-itnayn, yawm it-talaata, yawm il-arba9a, yawm il-khamiis, yawm il-jum9a, yawm is-sabt

3 • law samaHt, is-suubermarket maftuuH aymta?
- is-suubermarket maftuuH kull yawm.
- w-iS Saydaliyya maftuuHa kull yawm kamaan?
- laa', hiyya maftuuHa min yawm il-itnayn li yawm is-sabt.
- maktab il-bariid maftuuH il-yawm?
- laa', huwwa ma'fuul il-yawm. il-yawm yawm il-jum9a. maktab il-bariid maftuuH min yawm il-aHad li yawm il-khamiis.

The supermarket is open every day; chemist's Mon-Sat; post office open Sun-Thurs.

4 Post office isn't open today because it's Friday.

5 • law samaHt, il-matHaf maftuuH **kull** yawm?

- il-matHaf **ma'fuul** il-yawm, bass huwwa **maftuuH** bukra.
- wi il-Hadii'a?
- il-Hadii'a **maftuuHa** kull yawm.

Page 53

2 is-saa9a arba9a
is-saa9a itnayn
is-saa9a sitta
is-saa9a Hida9ashar
is-saa9a tamanya

3
- law samaHt, ayy saa9a b-yiftaH il-matHaf?
- huwwa maftuuH min is-saa9a tis9a lis-saa9a arba9a.

- law samaHti, ayy saa9a b-yiftaH il-maT9am?
- b-yiftaH is-saa9a sitta.
- wa ayy saa9a b-yi'fil?
- b-yi'fil is-saa9a 9ashara.

- law samaHt, ayy saa9a b-tiftaH il-maHaTTa?
- b-tiftaH is-saa9a khamsa, wa b-ti'fil is-saa9a tis9a.

a 9.00–4.00; b 6.00–10.00; c 5.00–9.00.

4 law samaHt, ayy saa9a b-yiftaH is-suu'?

Page 54

1 a 7; b 5; c 6; d 8; e 3; f 2; g 1; h 4

2 a il-matHaf maftuuH min yawm it-talaata li yawm il-khamiis. b-yiftaH is-saa9a tis9a. b-yi'fil is-saa9a khamsa.

b iS-Saydaliyya maftuuHa kull yawm. b-tiftaH is-saa9a tamanya. b-ti'fil is-saa9a sab9a.

c il-ba'aal maftuuH min yawm il-itnayn li yawm is-sabt. b-yiftaH is-saa9a 9ashara. b-yi'fil is-saa9a sitta.

Page 55

1
- **law samaHt, mumkin ti'uul li fiih maqha internet hawn?**

- aywa, fiih maqha internet mi'aabil il-bank.
- **wayn maT9am 9alaa' id-diin?**
- il-maT9am janb is-suu'.
- **shukran, ma9a as-salaama.**
- allaah yisalmak.

2
- **law samaHti, ayy saa9a b-yiftaH maktab il-bariid?**
- maktab il-bariid b-yiftaH is-saa9a tamanya.
- **huwwa maftuuH kull yawm?**
- laa', huwwa ma'fuul yawm il-aHad.
- **il-matHaf maftuuH il-yawm?**
- laa', huwwa ma'fuul il-yawm. il-matHaf maftuuH bukra.
- **shukran kitiir.**
- ahlan wa sahlan.

Page 56

1 yawm il-jum9a; 2 aymta, wayn; 3 maa fiih, maftuuH, b-yi'fil; 4 dakaakiin; 5 mi'aabil opposite; 6 waraa behind; 7 il-mustashfa; 8 maT9am il-fundu'

Unit 6

Page 60

2
- law samaHti, mumkin ti'uuli li kiif aruuH lis-suu'?
- **huwwa 9ala Tuul, fi aakhir ish-shaari9.**
- shukran kitiir.

a It's straight ahead; b at the end of the road.

3
- law samaHt, mumkin ti'uul li wayn **a'rab suubermarket**?
- **aasif, maa b-a9raf.**

- law samaHti, mumkin ti'uuli li wayn a'rab suubermarket?
- aywa, fiih suubermarket **fi taani shaari9 9al-yasaar.**
- shukran kitiir.

to the nearest supermarket; he doesn't know; it's on the second street on the left.

4 ● **law samaHti, kiif aruuH lil-bank?**

♦ **huwwa fi awwal shaari9 9al-yamiin, fi aakhir ish-shaari9.**

● shukran kitiir.

It's on the first street on the right, at the end of the road.

Page 61

2 ● ruuHi li ishaarat il-muruur. liffi yamiin. il-bank fi aakhir ish-shaari9.

♦ ruuHi 9ala Tuul, liffi yasaar wa ba9dayn khudi taani yamiin. il-matHaf 9al-yamiin.

● ruuHi li ishaarat il-muruur, liffi yamiin. khudi awwal yasaar. is-suu' mi'aabil il-fundu'.

1 museum; 2 market; 3 bank

3 ● law samaHt, kiif aruuH lil-jaami9a?

♦ liffi yasaar wa ba9dayn liffi yamiin, khudi taani yamiin. il-jaami9a fi awwal shaari9 9al-yamiin.

● law samaHti kiif aruuH lil-jaami9a?

♦ liffi yasaar wa ba9dayn liffi yamiin. khudi taani yasaar. il-jaami9a fi aakhir ish-shaari9.

The second person gave the right directions

Page 62

1 miyya wa waaHid, miyya wa itnayn, miyya wa 9ishriin, miyya wa khamsiin, miitayn, talatmiyya, arba9miyya, khamasmiyya, sittmiyya, sab9amiyya, tamanmiyya, tis9amiyya, alf, alfayn.

2 miyya wa talatiin, miitayn wa khamsiin, khamasmiyya wa tamaniin, sittmiyya wa arba9a wa talatiin, sab9amiyya wa waaHid wa saba9iin, tis9amiyya wa tis9a wa tis9iin.

4 ● mumkin taakhudni li fundu' Cedarland, law samaHt?

♦ Ce-dar-land? **maa b-a9raf wayn haada-l fundu'.**

● huwwa fi shaari9 9abd il-9aziiz.

♦ fil-Hamra?

● aywa, fil-Hamra. il-fundu' ba9iid min hawn?

● **ta'riiban talatiin da'ii'a.** … haadha shaari9 9abd il-9aziiz, ya akhi.

♦ Tayyib, il-Cedarland fi aakhir ish-shaari9 9al-yasaar, **Hawaali miitayn mitr** min hawn.

● itfaDDal. fundu' il-Cedarland!

♦ shukran kitiir.

a he doesn't know where the hotel is; b about 30 mins; c about 200m

5 ● law samaHt, fiih maqha il-internet hawn?

♦ aywa, fiih waaHid hawn.

● huwwa 'ariib?

♦ **Hawaali khamasmiit mitr.**

● shukran.

It's approx 500m away.

6 *a is-suu' 'ariib min hawn?;*
b mumkin taakhudni lil-jaami9a?

Page 63

2 ● law samaHti, mumkin ti'uuli li wayn maHaTTat il-qiTaar?

♦ maHaTTat il-qiTaar? khud taani yamiin.

● aasif, **mish faahim. marra taanya, min faDlik?**

♦ khud taani yamiin.

● **mumkin titkallami shway, shway,** min faDlik?

♦ aywa! khud … taani … yamiin.

● shukran kitiir.

b The railway station is on the second right.

3 ● ahlan. min wayn HaDirtik?

♦ mumkin titkallam shway, shway, min faDlak?

● min wayn HaDirtik?

♦ HaDirtak b-titkallam ingliizi?

● laa', b-atkallam 9arabi bass. ana

min il-urdun. min wayn inti?
- aah, ana faahma! ana min amriika. ismi Sarah.
- ahlan, ana ismi Abdallah.
- ahlan fiik. b-atkallam 9arabi shwayya.

Page 64

1 *a* 5; *b* 1; *c* 2; *d* 6; *e* 4; *f* 3

2 *a* ti'uul li; *b* a'rab; *c* aakhir; *d* 'ariib; *e* taani; *f* taakhudni; *g* khamasmiit

3 - law samaHt, kiif aruuH lil-matHaf?
- ruuHi 9ala Tuul, ba9dayn khudi awwal shaari9 9al-yamiin.
- mumkin marra taanya, min faDlak?
- ruuHi 9ala Tuul, ba9dayn khudi awwal shaari9 9al-yamiin.
- huwwa ba9iid?
- laa', mish ba9iid. Hawaali arba9miit mitr min hawn.
- shukran.
To the museum; go straight on then take the first road on the right; about 400m.

Page 65

1 - **law samaHt, wayn a'rab bank?**
- ta'riiban miitayn mitr min hawn 9al-yasaar.
- **mumkin marra taanya, min faDlak?**
- ta'riiban miitayn mitr min hawn 9al-yasaar.
- **shukran, ma9a as-salaama.**
- allah yisalmak.

2 - **law samaHti, HaDirtik b-tikallami ingliizi?**
- laa', maa b-atkallam ingliizi.
- **kiif aruuH li maHaTTat il-qiTaar min hawn?**
- ruuHi 9ala Tuul, ba9dayn khudi taani shaari9 9al-yamiin, wa maHaTTat il-qiTaar fi aakhir ish-shaari9.
- **asfa, mish faahma.**
- ruuHi 9ala Tuul, ba9dayn khudi

taani shaari9 9al-yamiin.
- **Tayyib, ruuHi 9ala Tuul, ba9dayn khudi taani shaari9 9al-yamiin. hiyya ba9iida?**
- shwayya, mish ba9iida kitiir – ta'riiban kilomitr waaHid min hawn.
- **shukran kitiir.**
- 9afwan.

Page 66

1 right; 2 ba9iid; 3 aruuH;
4 khamasmiit mitr 500m; 5 mumkin marra taanya, min faDlak; *6 slowly;*
7 asfa, maa b-a9raf; *8 I don't speak French.*

Unit 7

Page 70

2 - ahlan wa sahlan.
- ahlan fiiki.
- mumkin ashuuf haada-l isharb?
- aywa, itfaDDali.
- 9andak alwaan taanya?
- 9andi **aHmar** wa **akhDar** wa **abyaD**.
- 9andak **aSfar**?
- aasif, maa 9andi.
red, green, white, yellow

3 - marHaba. mumkin ashuuf haada-l 'amiiS, law samaHt?
- il-'amiiS il-aswad?
- aywa, mumkin a'iisu?
- Tab9an, itfaDDal.
- mmm … Saghiir shwayya. 9andak ma'aas akbar?
- laa', aasif, maa 9andi 'amiiS kibiir aswaD.
a false, he wants a black shirt; b true;
c true.

4 - marHaba. mumkin ashuuf haadi-sh shanTa **iz-zar'a**, min faDlik?
- itfaDDali.
- mmm, kibiira shwayya, wa maa b-aHibb il-lawn.
- Tayyib, b-tHibbi haadi-sh shanTa **il-Hamra**? itfaDDali, shuufi.

- laa', maa b-aHibb il-lawn **il-aHmar.**
- Tayyib, shuufi haadi-sh shanTa **il-khaDra.**
- aywa, haadi-sh shanTa il-khaDra Hilwa kitiir.

She likes the green handbag.

2 • law samaHti, 'addaysh **il-jakayt?**
- haada **bi khamsa wa arba9iin dinaar.**
- wa 'addaysh haadi-**l bluuza** iz-zar'a?
- haadi **bi talatiin dinaar.**
- Tayyib, 'addaysh haada?
- **il-fustaan bi miyya wa saba9iin dinaar.**
- haada ghaali kitiir!
- b-a9raf, haada-l fustaan min fransa!
- 9andik shi arkhas?

a 30 dinar; b 170 dinar; c 45 dinar.

3 The dress is from France.

4 • 'addaysh haadi-l jariida il-ingliiziyya?
- il-jariida bi tamaniin lira.
- wa 'addaysh haadi-l majalla?
- il-majalla bi tis9iin lira.
- 9andak kuruut?
- 9andi, hadawl bi 9ishriin lira.
- Tayyib, wa haada-l kitaab 'addaysh?
- haada bi miitayn lira.
- w-9andak Tawaabi9?
- mumkin tiruuH li maktab il-bariid.
- shukran.

a postcards; b English newspaper; c magazine; d book. Stamps aren't available; he must go to the post office.

5 haadi-sh shanTa ghaalya kitiir. 'addaysh hadawl il-kutub?

2 • fiih **tawaabil** mumtaaza hawn.
- laa' shukran. 9andi tawaabil kitiir fil-bayt.
- haadi-S **SuHuun** Hilwa.
- mumkin ashuufha? aywa, Hilwa kitiir.
- wi hawn fiih **Sawaani** Hilwa, wa **fanaajiin** mumtaaza kamaan.
- laa', maa biddi. laakin biddi **ibrii' shaay.**
- haada ibrii' shaay mumtaaz.
- mumkin ashuufu?
- itfaDDali.

3 • mumkin ashuuf haada **ibrii' ish-shaay,** law samaHt?
- itfaDDali.
- 'addaysh haada?
- haada bi talaatmiit lira.
- haada ghaali kitiir. mumkin ashuuf haadi-S **Siniyya,** law samaHt?
- aywa, itfaDDali.
- 'addaysh haadi?
- haadi bi miitayn lira.
- Tayyib, b-aakhudha.
- biddik shi taani?
- bass iS-Siniyya, shukran.

teapot, tray. She buys the tray.

4 • SabaaH il-khayr. mumkin ashuuf hadawl il-fanaajiin?
- itfaDDal, 'addaysh biddak?
- b-aakhud 9ashara min hadawl.
- Tayyib. wa biddak shi taani?
- mumkin ashuuf haada-S SaHn, law samaHt?
- 'addaysh biddak?
- biddi talaata, min faDlak.
- HaaDir, shi taani?
- aywa, 9andak ibrii' 'ahwa?
- itfaDDal.
- ana b-aHibbu. b-aakhdu.

10 cups, 3 dishes, one coffee pot.

2 • law samaHt, 'addaysh ibrii' il-'ahwa?
- bi talatmiyya wa khamsiin lira.
- haada ghaali kitiir. miitayn lira mniiH?
- laa', mish mumkin, aasif ya madaam.

- Tayyib, shuu aHsan taman 9andak?
- miitayn wa khamsa wa saba9iin lira.
- laa', laa', haada ghaali. itfaDDal miitayn wa khamsiin lira.
- HaaDir, 9ashaanik ya madaam, bi miitayn wa khamsiin lira.

a 350 Syrian pounds; b 250 Syrian pounds

3 9ashaanik ya madaam *for you madam*

4
- itfaDDal, itfaDDal, ya akhi. shuu biddak **tishtiri?**
- biddi **ashuuf** bass.
- haada-S SaHn jamiil kitiir.
- laa', shukran, maa biddi **ashtiri.**
- iS-Siniyya bi miitayn lira bass!
- miyya wa khamsiin lira **mniiH?**
- laa', mish mumkin.
- shuu **aHsan** taman 9andak?
- miyya wa saba9iin lira.
- **b-aakhudha.**

Page 74

1 *a* Siniyya *tray, the rest are items of clothing; b* rakhiiS *cheap, the rest are used to make comparisons; c* miyya *a hundred, the rest are currencies; d* akbar *bigger, the rest are colours.*

2 *a* iz-zar'a; *b* il-aswad; *c* il-Hilwa; *d* kibiir; *e* il-aHmar; *f* akbar; *g* arkhaS; *h* mumtaaz.

3 *a* ashuufu; *b* ashtiri; *c* b-aakhudha; *d* haada-l; *e* b-aakhudha; *f* hadawl il-.

Page 75

1
- ahlan, SabaaH il-khayr.
- **SabaaH in-nuur. 'addaysh haada-l 'amiiS il-abyaD?**
- il-'amiiS bi miyya wa 9ishriin lira.
- **mumkin a'iisu?**
- itfaDDal.
- **Saghiir shwayya. 9andak ma'aas akbar?**
- laa', maa 9andi.

2
- marHaba, ahlan wa sahlan. itfaDDal.
- **law samaHti, 'addaysh haadi-sh shanTa?**
- haadi bi tis9amiit lira suuriyya.
- **9andik shanTa Hamra?**
- 9andi bass aswad wa azra'.
- **Tayyib, b-aakhud ish-shanTa iz-zar'a.**

3
- aywa, ayy khidma?
- **mumkin ashuuf haadi-S Siniyya?**
- itfaDDal.
- **'addaysh haadi?**
- haadi bi miitayn lira.
- **haadi ghaalya kitiir. miyya wa 9ishriin mniiH?**
- laa', mish mumkin.
- **shuu aHsan taman 9andak?**
- miyya wa sittiin kwayyis?
- **itfaDDal, miyya wa khamsiin lira.**
- Tayyib, itfaDDal.

Page 76

1 the dish is beautiful, the beautiful dish; 2 miitayn riyaal *is more as it is 200 (*itnayn riyaal *is 2); 3* aTwal; *4* kitiir; *5 colour; 6* biddi khamsa min hadawl; *7* aSghar 'amiiS; *8* Hamra; *9* b-aakhudha; *10* kuruut taanya.

Checkpoint 2

Pages 77–80

1
- maT9am kababji fi shaari9 il-Hamra mish ba9iid min hawn, Hawaali khamsa da'aayi' min il-fundu'.
- il-jaami9a il-amriikiyya 'ariiba kitiir min il-fundu' fi aakhir haada-sh shaari9! Hawaali khamasmiit mitr min hawn.
- il-matHaf il-waTani ba9iid shwayya min hawn, janb fundu' is-safiir, Hawaali 9ishriin da'ii'a min hawn bit-taksi.

a in il-Hamra *street, not far from here, about 5 minutes from the hotel; b very*

Transcripts and answers **125**

near the hotel, at the end of the road, about 500m away; c quite far, next to Hotel is-safiir, about 20 minutes away by taxi.

2 ● maT9am kababji maftuuH kull yawm min is-saa9a waaHda lis-saa9a Hida9sh.
  ● il-jaami9a il-amriikiyya maftuuHa min yawm il-itnayn li yawm il-jum9a.
  ● il-matHaf il-waTani ma'fuul kull yawm aHad.
maT9am kababji: open every day from 1-11; il-jaami9a il-amriikiyya: open Mon–Fri; il-matHaf il-waTani: closed every Sun.

3 *a* 6; *b* 7; *c* 1; *d* 5; *e* 4; *f* 9; *g* 10; *h* 8; *i* 3; *j* 2

4 ibrii', finjaan, Siniyya; fustaan, isharb, 'amiiS; matHaf, maHaTTa, maktab bariid; 9ala Tuul, 9al yasaar, 9al yamiin; ruuH, liff, khud; miitayn, talatmiyya, arba9miyya; mi'aabil, janb, waraa.

5 *a* 5; *b* 7; *c* 2; *d* 6; *e* 3; *f* 4; *g* 1

6 ● **ibri il-'ahwa** bi sittmiyya wa khamsiin lira.
  ● **il-jariida il-ingiiziyya** bi miyya wa talatiin lira.
  ● **sitt fanaajiin** bi khamasmiit lira.
  ● **Siniyya 9arabiyya** bi saba9miit lira.
  ● **'amiiS** bi khamsmiyya wa talatiin lira.
  ● **il-isharb** bi talatmiyya wa arba9iin lira.
coffee pot 650 lira; English newspaper 130 lira; 6 cups 500 lira; Arabic tray 700 lira; shirt 530 lira; scarf 340 lira.

7 *a* HaDirtak/HaDirtik b-titkallam/b-titkallami ingliizi?; *b* mumkin ti'uuli/ti'uuli li wayn a'rab Saydaliyya?; *c* il-maHaTTa 'ariiba min hawn?; *d* ayy saa9a b-yiftaH il-bank?; *e* 'addaysh haada?; *f* fiih suubermarket hawn?

8 *1* ghaalya; *2* mniiH; *3* a'iis; *4* aHsan; *5* kiif; *6* liff; *7* khud

9 ● law samaHti, mumkin ti'uuli li wayn il-maHaTTa il-kibiira?
  ◆ na9am – bass hiyya ba9iida shwayya. khud awwal yamiin wa ba9dayn ruuH 9ala Tuul wa khud taani shaari9 9al-yamiin. il-maHaTTa 9al-yasaar.
  ● shukran.

  ● law samaHt, wayn fundu' riyaaD is-salaam?
  ◆ fundu' riyaaD is-salaam? mish ba9iid min hawn. liffi yasaar ba9dayn khudi awwal yamiin wa ba9ayn taani yamiin. w-il fundu' 9al-yasaar.
  ● shukran kitiir.

  ● wayn maktab il-bariid?
  ◆ maktab il-bariid? min Café France liffi yasaar, ruuHi 9ala Tuul wa maktab il-bariid 9al-yamiin mi'aabil il-qunSuliyya il-fransiyya.
  ● shukran.

  ● mumkin ti'tuul li wayn is-suu'?
  ◆ na9am … is suu' waraa baab marraaksh.
  ● wayn baab marraaksh?
  ◆ shuuf! baab marraaksh mish ba9iid. ruuH yamiin wa ba9dayn khud taani shaari9 9al-yasaar wa baab marraaksh 9al-yamiin. is-suu' waraa baab marraaksh.
1 Hotel Riyaad salaam; 2 the market; 3 the post office; 4 the big station

10 *1* c; *2* d; *3* a; *4* b

11 *a* 2; *b* 1; *c* 3; *d* 3; *e* 2; *f* 1; *g* 3; *h* 1; *i* 2

Unit 8
Page 82

2 ● marHaba!
  ◆ marHabtayn. 9andik ghurfa?
  ● li kam shakhS?

- li shakhSayn. **biddi ghurfa li shakhSayn bi Hammaam**, min faDlik.

- marHaba!
- marHabtayn. **biddi ghurfa li talaat ashkhaaS**, min faDlik.
- Tayyib. 9andi ghurfa **biduun Hammaam**.
- b-aakhudha. shukran.

- ahlan wa sahlan. 9andak ghurfa?
- ahlan fiik, li kam shakhS?
- li shakhSayn. **biddi ghurfa li shakhSayn bi takyiif**.

- SabaaH il-khayr.
- SabaaH in-nuur.
- **biddi ghurfa li shakhS waaHid bi Hammaam**, min faDlik.

Double room with bathroom; room for three people without bathroom; double room with air-conditioning; single room with bathroom.

3 • Tayyib, il-ghurfa li shakhSayn bi Hammaam 'addaysh il-layla, law samaHti?
- **bi fuTuur bi talatmiit lira** il-layla.
- wa biduun fuTuur?
- **biduun fuTuur bi miitayn wa khamsiin lira.**

With breakfast 300 Syrian pounds, without 250 Syrian pounds.

Page 83

2 • li kam layla, ya madaam?
- biddi anzil **layltayn**.

- aymta biddak tinzil?
- **min il-yawm li yawm it-talaata.**

- ya aanisa, biddik tinzili li kam layla?
- biddi anzil **haadi-l layla bass**.

3 • is-salaam 9alaykum. il-fundu' il-umawi … aloo.
- ahlan wa sahlan. biddi ghurfa li

shakhS waaHid, min faDlik.
- li kam layla?
- biddi anzil layltayn, **min yawm waaHid sitta li talaata sitta.**
- aywa, fiih ghurfa. il-ism, min faDlak?

- is-salaam 9alaykum, il-fundu' il-umawi. ayy khidma?
- ahlan wa sahlan. 9andik ghurfa li shakSayn?
- aymta biddik tinzili?
- biddi il-ghurfa **haadi-l layla bass**.
- asfa, **il fundu' kullu maHjuuz.**

- is-salaam 9alaykum. il-fundu' il-umawi. ayy khidma?
- wa 9alaykum is-salaam. biddi ghurfa **min yawm arba9a tis9a li yawm sitta tis9a**. mumkin?
- aywa, mumkin.

a 1–3 June; b just for tonight (hotel is full); c 4–6 September.

Page 84

2 • ahlan wa sahlan. ana ismi Maryam Munir. 9andi Hajz.
- maa fiih Hajz bi ismik. Hajazti aymta?
- Hajazt imbaariH.
- li kam shakhS?
- **li shakhSayn**.
- li kam layla?
- biddi anzil **talaat layaali**.
- biddik ghurfa bi Hammaam?
- Tab9an!
- Tayyib, **imli il-istimaara**, min faDlik.
- itfaDDal.
- itfaDDali il-muftaaH. **ghurfa raqm miitayn wa 9ashara.**
- shukran.

a double with bath; b three nights; c to fill in the form; d 210.

3 The receptionist didn't have a booking in her name.

4 • marHaba.
- marHabtayn. 9andi Hajz. **ismi**

Patrick Murphy.

- inta Hajazt ghurfa li shakhSayn, **min yawm itnaa9sh talaata li sitta9sh talaata?**
- aywa.
- jawaaz safarak, min faDlak.
- itfaDDali.
- Tayyib. **jawaaz raqm: Sifr, Sifr, khamsa, itnayn, khamsa, tis9a,sitta, arba9a. il-jinsiyya: irlandi.** itfaDDal il-muftaaH. HaDirtak fi **ghurfa raqm tis9a wa khamsiin, fiT-Taabi' it-taalit.**
- shukran. law samaHti, wayn il-asinsiir?
- **il-asinsiir mi'aabil il-maT9am.**
- shukran.

Patrick Murphy, from 12 to 16 March, passport no. 00525964, Irish, room 59. a third floor; b opposite the restaurant.

Page 85

2
- SabaaH il-khayr.
- SabaaH in-nuur, ya aanisa Maryam. ayy khidma?
- law samaHt, **mumkin tuTlub taksi 9ashaani?**
- Tab9an mumkin. ayy khidma taanya?
- aywa, **mumkin akhalli shanTati hawn?**
- akiid.

a she wants him to call a taxi; b to leave her suitcase; it means anything else?

3
- ya madaam Campbell, itfaDDali il-Hisaab.
- **mumkin adfa9 bi haada-l kart?**
- Tab9an mumkin.

- ahlan, ya Hasan.
- ahlan, ya duktuur Rushdi.
- **mumkin asta9mil Hammaam is-sibaaHa?**
- Tab9an, huwwa fiT-Taabi' it-taalit.

- law samaHt.
- aywa, ya sayyid Ramzi?
- **mumkin akhalli shanTati hawn?**
- aywa, akiid.

- ahlan wa sahlan, ya aanisa Buthayna. itfaDDali il-muftaaH.
- ahlan fiik. law samaHt, **mumkin ashuuf il-mudiir?**
- laa', aasif. mish mumkin il-yawm.
  il-mudiir f-iskandariyya!

Mrs Campbell: pay with this card; Dr Rushdi: use the swimming pool; Mr Ramzi: leave his suitcase; Miss Buthayna: see the manager.

4 Miss Buthayna's; the manager is in Alexandria.

Page 86

1 *a* 9andik ghurfa?; *b* bi takyiif? *c* biddi anzil haadi-l layla bass; *d* 9andi Hajz; *e* 'addaysh il-layla?; *f* mumkin asta9mil Hammaan is-sibaaHa?; *g* Hajazt imbaariH.

2 *a* shakhS waaHid; *b* shakSayn bi Hammaam; *c* takyiif; *d* tuTlub taksi; *e* asta9mil il-internet.

3 *a* yawm waaHid wa talatiin waaHid; *b* yawm arba9a wa 9ishriin itna9sh; *c* yawm khamsa talaata; *d* yawm tamanya sab9a.

Page 87

1
- marHaba, ayy khidma?
- **9andak ghurfa?**
- biddak tinzil li kam layla?
- **layla waaHda bass.**
- li shakhS waaHid?
- **laa', li shakhSayn wa bi Hammaam, min faDlak.**
- aywa, fiih ghurfa bi sab9iin dinaar il-layla.
- **bi fuTuur?**
- aywa, bi fuTuur.

2
- SabaaH il-khayr.
- **SabaaH in-nuur.**

- ayy khidma?
- **il-Hisaab, min faDlik.**
- raqm il-ghurfa, law samaHt?
- **ghurfa raqm miitayn wa 9ashara.**
- saba9iin dinaar, min faDlak.
- **mumkin adfa9 bi haada-l kart?**
- aywa, Tab9an.
- **mumkin akhalli shanTati hawn lis-saa9a arba9a il-yawm?**
- aywa, akiid. b-ashuufak ba9dayn.
- **ma9a as-salaama.**

1 ghurfa; 2 biddi anzil arba9a layaali; 3 yawm sab9a 9ashara; 4 the manager; 5 ghurfa bi takyiif; 6 mumkin tuTlub taksi 9ashaani; 7 fill in the form; 8 the key; 9 biddi ghurfatayn.

Unit 9

2
- law samaHt, biddi aruuH li ba9albak. kiif mumkin aruuH min hawn?
- HaDritak raayiH aymta?
- raayiH bukra.
- mumkin tiruuH bil **baaS** wa mumkin taakhud **taksi** kamaan.
- mumkin aakhud il-qiTaar?
- laa', mish mumkin. maa fiih qiTaaraat fi lubnaan!

bus, taxi; there aren't any trains in Lebanon.

3
- SabaaH il-khayr.
- SabaaH in-nuur.
- raayiH lil-maTaar bukra. mumkin aakhud il-baaS min hawn?
- laa', maa fiih baaS lil-maTaar. laazim taakhud taksi.
- 'addaysh it-taksi min hawn lil-maTaar?
- Hawaali arba9iin dinaar.
- haada ghaali kitiir!

4 biddi aruuH lil-matHaf; mumkin aakhud il-baaS?

2
- law samaHt, haada-l baaS b-yruuH lil-jaami9 il-umawi?
- laa', haada-l baaS lil-jaami9a.
- Tayyib, ayy raqm baaS b-yruuH li- jaami9 il-umawi?
- laazim taakhdi baaS raqm itnayn wa 9ishriin.
- 'addaysh b-yaakhud?
- Hawaali 9ashar da'aayi' bass.
- wa fiih baaS min hawn lil-maTaar?
- na9am, fiih ya madaam.
- ayy raqm?
- miyya.

a true; b false, bus no. 22; c false, it takes 10 minutes; d false, bus no.100 goes to the airport.

3
- law samaHt, fiih baaS li Halab min hawn?
- aywa, fiih.
- 'addaysh b-yaakhud?
- **b-yaakhud Hawaali khams saa9aat.**
- min wayn b-yruuH?
- min hunaak, 9al-yasaar.
- ----------------
- law samaHti, haada-l baaS b-yruuH li 9ammaan?
- aywa.
- 'addaysh b-taakhud ir-riHla?
- **ir-riHla b-taakhud Hawaali arba9a saa9aat.**
- wa 'addaysh b-taakhud ir-riHla li Homs?
- **Hawaali saa9atayn.**
- min wayn b-yruuH?
- min hunaak, 9al-yamiin.
- shukran, ya madaam.

a 5 hours; b 4 hours; c 2 hours

4 *Aleppo:* min hunaak, 9al-yasaar *from over there, on the left; Homs:* min hunaak 9al-yamiin *from over there, on the right.*

2
- **biddi arba9a tazaakir li dimashq,** min faDlik.

- ◆ daraja uula aw daraja taanya?
- ● **daraja uula,** min faDlik.
- ◆ biddak tazkarat ruuHa aw ruuHa raj9a?
- ● **ruuHa bass,** law samaHti.
- ◆ biddak lil-yawm?
- ● laa', **li bukra.**
- ◆ Tayyib. arba9a tazaakir ruuHa li dimashq daraja uula. **il-majmuu9 talaat alaaf wa khamasmiit lira min faDlak.**
- ● itfaDDali. wa min ayy raSiif?
- ◆ **raSiif raqm sitta.**
- ● shukran.

4 single first class tickets to Damascus for tomorrow. Total 3,500 Syrian pounds.

3 platform number 6

4 ● biddi **tazkarat ruuHa lir-ribaaT**, min faDlak. 'addaysh it-tazkara?
- ◆ **khamsa wa 9ishriin dirham**, min faDlak.

- ● biddi **tazkartayn ruuHa raj9a lil-jadiida,** law samaHt.
- ◆ lil-jadiida? **khamsa wa arba9iin dirham.**

- ● **talaat tazaakir ruuHa li faas**, min faDlik.
- ◆ **miyya wa 9ishriin dirham.**
- ● shukran.

- ◆ **il-maTaar**, min faDlak.
- ● ruuHa aw ruuHa raj9a?
- ◆ **ruuHa bass,** law samaHt.
- ● **itnaa9shar dirham**, min faDlik.
- ◆ itfaDDal.

a 25 dirhams; b 45 dirhams; c 120 dirhams; d 12 dirhams.

Page 95

2 ● law samaHt, ayy saa9a il-qiTaar li Tanja?
- ◆ il-qiTaar il-jaay **b-yimshi ba9d rub9 saa9a.**
- ● ya9ni **is-saa9a Hidaa9shar wa nuSS?**
- ◆ aywa, Hidaa9ashar wa nuSS.

- ● wa ayy saa9a b-yuSal Tanja?
- ◆ **is-saa9a arba9a illa rub9.**
- ● shukran.

a 11.30; b a quarter of an hour; c 3.45

3 ● ayy saa9a il-qiTaar il-jaay li marraaksh?
- ◆ ba9d nuSS saa9a. **is-saa9a talaata wa 9ashara.**
- ● wa aymta b-yuSal li marraaksh?
- ◆ **b-yuSal is-saa9a sitta.**

- ● ya ukhti, il-qiTaar li Tanja b-yimshi ayy saa9a?
- ◆ **b-yimshi is-saa9a arba9a illa rub9.**
- ● wa aymta b-yuSal Tanja?
- ◆ **b-yuSal Tanja is-saa9a khamsa wa tult.**
- ● shukran.

- ● law samaHti, aymta il-qiTaar il-jaay lil-jadiida?
- ◆ il-jadiida? ba9d saa9a – **is-saa9a sab9a wa 9ashara. b-yuSal il-jadiida is-saa9a tis9a wa nuSS.**
- ● shukran.

Marrakesh 3.10, 6.00; Tangiers 3.45, 5.20; Al-Jadida 7.10, 9.30.

4 aymta il-qiTaar il-jaay lir-ribaaT?

Page 96

1 *a* 2; *b* 5; *c* 6; *d* 1; *e* 4; *f* 3

2 *a* is-saa9a sab9a wa nuSS;
b is-saa9a waaHda illa rub9;
c is-saa9a itnayn wa rub9;
d is-saa9a talaata wa nuSS illa khamsa; *e* is-saa9a arba9a wa tult;
f is-saa9a 9ashara illa 9ashara.

3 *1* b-yuSal; *2* aakhud; *3* b-yimshi; *4*; b-taakhud; *5* taakhdi; *6* tiruuH

4 *a* 6; *b* 4; *c* 5; *d* 2; *e* 3; *f* 1

Page 97

1 ● **fiih baaS li dimashq?**
- ◆ aywa, fiih baaS li dimashq kull yawm is-saa9a talaata.
- ● **'addaysh b-taakhud ir-riHla?**

- ir-riHla b-taakhud Hawaali arba9a saa9aat min 9amman li dimashq.
- **'addaysh it-tazkara?**
- biddak tazkarat ruuHa aw ruuHa raj9a?
- **biddi tazkartayn ruuHa bass, min faDlik.**
- Tayyib, haada khamsiin dinaar, min faDlak.
- **itfaDDali.**
- shukran.

2 • **aymta b-yimshi il-qiTaar il-jaay li Halab?**
- b-yimshi is-saa9a tamanya wa nuSS.
- **aymta b-yusal il-qiTaar Halab?**
- b-yuSal is-saa9a itnaa9sh wa nuSS.
- **biddi tazkarat ruuHa raj9a.**
- daraja taanya aw daraja uula?
- **daraja uula, min faDlak. 'addaysh?**
- tamanmiit lira.
- **'addaysh daraja taanya?**
- sittmiyya wa khamsiin lira.
- **biddi tazkara waaHda – ruuHa raj9a daraja uula, min faDlak.**
- itfaDDal. riHla sa9iida.
- **shukran. il-qiTaar b-yruuH min ayy raSiif?**
- raSiif raqm itnayn.

Page 98

1 8.40; 2 riHla; 3 ruuHa raj9a daraja taanya; *4 four o'clock and four hours; 5 next; 6 railway station; 7 tazkartayn; 8 You must take a taxi and You can take a taxi.*

Unit 10
Page 102

1 • il-yawm min il-muqabbilaat 9andnaa: tabbuuleh, wa fuul, wa mutabbal; wa min il-mashwiyyaat 9andnaa dajaaj mashwi, wa kibda mashwiyya, wa samak mashwi wa kufta mashwiyya. lil Hilu 9andnaa

umm 9ali, wa kunaafa, wa ba'laawa il-yawm.
Not mentioned: falaafil; mashwi mishakkal, krim karamil, ruzz bi Haliib.

2 • itfaDDali. shuu b-tHibbi?
- **waaHid kufta mashwiyya wa waaHid samak mashwi**, law samaHt.
- HaDirtik biddik muqabbilaat?
- mmm … ya Hiba, biddik muqabbilaat?
- aywa, aywa,Tab9an! biddi tabbuuleh, min faDlik.
- Tayyib, **waaHid mutabbal** wa **waaHid tabbuuleh**.
- HaaDir, ya madaam.
Farida orders 1 grilled meat, 1 grilled fish, 1 smoked aubergine dip and 1 crushed wheat and parsley salad.

3 • law samaHt, **9andkum krim karamil** il-yawm?
- laa', maa fiih.
- Tayyib, **b-aakhud ba'laawa,** min faDlak.
She wants crème caramel, she orders baklava.

Page 103

2 • ya Mark, b-tHibb il-falaafil wa-l kibbeh?
- **b-aHibb il-kibbeh**, bass **maa b-aHibb il-falaafil**.
- Tayyib, b-taakul laHma?
- laa', **maa b-aHibb il-laHma**. ana maa b-aakul laHma abadan.
- b-tHibb is-samak il-mashwi?
- aywa, **b-aHibb is-samak**, b-aHibbu kitiir.
- wa b-tHibb il-ba'laawa?
- aywa, **b-aHibbha** Tab9an! bass **b-afaDDil il-kunaafa**.
falaafil ✗; kibbeh ✓; laHma ✗; samak mashwi ✓; ba'laawa ✓; kunaafa ✓.

3 • ya Jaqueline, **b-tHibbi** il-kufta il-mashwiyya?
- ya9ni, mish kitiir, **b-afaDDil** id-dajaaj.
- w-inta, ya David, **b-tHibb** il-kufta il-mashwiyya?

- laa', ana nabaati, maa b-aakul laHma **abadan**!
- Tayyib, **b-taakul** salaaTaat lubnaaniyya?
- Tab9an, **b-aHibbha** kitiir.

nabaati vegetarian.

Page 104

2 • ya garsawn!
- aywa, ya ustaaz? shuu b-taakhud?
- biddi **itnayn dajaaj mashwi**, wa **waaHid kibda mashwiyya**, wa **talaata mashwi mishakkal**, law samaHt. aah, wa ayy naw9 akl nabaati 9andkum?
- fiih mujaddara.
- Tayyib, **waaHid mujaddara** kamaan.
- wa HaDirtak biddak muqabbilaat?
- aywa, biddi **arba9a mutabbal** wa **itnayn SalSat TaHiina**, law samaHt.
- Tayyib, waaHid mujaddara, itnayn dajaaj mashwi, waaHid kibda mashwiyya, wa talaata mashwi mishakkal, w-il muqabbilaat – arba9a mutabbal wa itnayn TaHiina.
- aywa maZbuuT. **mumkin kamaan khubz**, law samaHt?
- HaaDir, ya ustaaz.

dajaaj mashwi *2*; kibda mashwiyya *1*; mashwi mishakkal *3*; mutabbal *4*; SalSat TaHiina *2*; mujaddara *1*. *He asks for more bread.*

3 • ahlan wa sahlan.
- ahlan fiiki. biddna Taawila li itnayn.
- itfaDDalu.
- ya aanisa. mumkin il-lista, law samaHti?
- itfaDDalu.
- ya Khalid, **il-akl hawn kwayyis kitiir**. ana b-aakhud il-kufta!
- ana b-aHibb il-kufta kamaan, ya Nadia.
- Tayyib, itnayn kufta mashwiyya,

min faDlik. ayy naw9 Hilu 9andkum?
- 9andnaa **ruzz bi Haliib** wa **ba'laawa**.
- 9andkum umm 9ali?
- laa', **maa 9andnaa umm 9ali il-yawm**.
- Tayyib, biddak ruzz bi Haliib, ya Khalid?
- maa biddi Hilu, shukran.
- biddik shi taani?
- **haada kullu.**
- HaaDir.

a She says that the food is very good. b She suggests ruzz bi Haliib *(rice pudding) and* ba'laawa. *c There is no* umm 9ali *(milk pudding) today. d* haada kullu

4 ayy naw9 fawaakih 9andkum?; biddi itnayn mashwi mishakkal, min faDlak; b-aakhud waaHid mutabbal wa waaHid mujaddara, min faDlak.

Page 105

2 • kiif kaan il-akl, ya Jacqueline?
- **il-akl kaan laziiz jiddan.**
- w-inta ya David, il-akl kaan kwayyis?
- il-akl kaan laziiz jiddan, **khuSuuSan is-samak**.
- **il khidma kaanat mumtaaza fi9lan!** shukran kitiir, ya Farida.
- **biddik taakli hawn marra taanya?**
- Tab9an. b-aHibb il-akl il-lubnaani kitiir!

1 David especially liked the fish; 2 Jacqueline was impressed with the food and the service; 3 Farida asks if she would like to eat here again.

3 • is-salaam 9alaykum ana mudiir il-maT9am.
- wa 9alaykum is-salaam.
- kiif kaan il-akl?
- **il-akl kaan laziiz, shukran.**
- **khuSuuSan il-laHma il-mashwiyya.**

- wa kiif kaanat il-khidma?
- **il-khidma kaanat mumtaaza.**
- w-il garsawn?
- **il-garsawn kaan laTiif jiddan.**

4 il-akl kaan laziiz, khuSuuSan id-dajaaj il-mashwi.

Page 106

1 *a* 6; *b* 5; *c* 2; *d* 3; *e* 1; *f* 4

2 *a* b-aHibbu; *b* b-aakulha; *c* b-aHibbha; *d* b-aaklu; *e* b-aakhdu; *f* b-aakhudha

3 *a* 2; *b* 8; *c* 1; *d* 3; *e* 4; *f* 6; *g* 5; *h* 7

Page 107

1 ◆ **biddna Taawila li itnayn.**
- itfaDDalu.
- ◆ **ayy naw9 akl nabaati 9andkum?**
- 9andnaa salaaTaat kitiir Tab9an.
- ◆ **Tayyib, biddi waaHid mutabbal wa waaHid tabbuuleh.**
- wa biddak mashwiyyaat?
- ◆ **b-aakhud waaHid mashwi mishakkal, law samaHt.**
- HaDirtak biddak shi taani?
- ◆ **mumkin kamaan khubz, law samaHt?**
- HaaDir, ya ustaaz.

2 ● ahlan wa sahlan, ana mudiir il-maT9am. kiif kaan il-akl?
- ◆ **il-akl kaan laziiz fi9lan.**
- kiif kaanat il-muqabbilaat?
- ◆ **il-muqabbilaat kaanat laziiza jiddan, khuSuuSan il-fuul!**
- wa kiif kaanat il-khidma?
- ◆ **il-khidma kaanat mumtaaza, w-il garsawn kaan laTiif jiddan.**
- shukran kitiir. marra taanya, in-shaa' allaah?
- ◆ **aywa, in-shaa' allaah.**

Page 108

1 yes; 2 biddna Taawila li-talaata; *3* kunaafa *is the odd one out as it is a dessert, the others tend to be starters; 4 more bread; 5* mumtaaza; *6* maa

b-ashrab biira abadan; *7* kiif kaan il-akl?; *8* shuu akalt imbaariH?

Checkpoint 3
Pages 109–112

1 *c*

2 ● mumkin jawaaz safarak, min faDlak?
- imla il-istimaara, law samaHt?
- HaDirtak fi ghurfa raqm talatmiyya wa arba9ta9sh.
- itfaDDal il-muftaaH.
- ghurftak fiT-Taabi' it-taalit.

1 your passport, please; 2 can you fill in this form, please; 3 you're in room 314; 4 here's the key; 5 your room is on the 3rd floor.

3 ● yawm it-talaata, bukra ya9ni, ana laazim aruuH lil-mustashfa ashuuf abi, wa ba9dayn biddi aruuH li ba9albak ashuuf ummi yawm il-arba9a.
- ◆ kam yawm biddak tinzil hunaak?
- li yawmayn. yawm il-jum9a laazim aruuH li dimashq lish-shughl, bass layla waaHda.
- biddak tiruuH li London min dimashq aw min bayruut?
- min bayruut. 9andi Hajz yawm il-aHad li London. b-aakhud taksi min dimashq li bayruut is-sabt.
- ◆ riHla sa9iida, ya Khalid.
- shukran, ya Nadia.

Tues: see father in hospital; Weds: to Baalbek to see mother; Thurs: Baalbek; Fri: to Damascus on business; Sat: taxi Damascus – Beirut; Sun: fly to London.

4 ● il-qiTaar li-Tanja b-yimshi ba9d nuSS saa9a.
- ◆ riHla raqm khamsa Sifr arba9a li dubay b-tiruuH ba9d saa9a.
- biddak ghurfa bi Hammaam?
- asfa, maa 9andnaa akl nabaati.
- Hammaam is-sibaaHa fiT-Taabi' il-awwal.
- ◆ biddak daraja uula aw daraja taanya?

- min wayn b-aakhud il-baaS li 9ammaan?
- il-maTaar ba9iid min haada-l fundu'. khud taksi – aHsan.

1 train station; 2 airport; 3 hotel reception; 4 restaurant; 5 hotel reception; 6 train station; 7 bus station; 8 hotel reception.

5 *a* law samaHt, mumkin asta9mil il-internet?; *b* law samaHt, kiif aruuH lil jaami9 il-umawi?; *c* law samaHt, wayn mumkin ashtiri jariida ingliiziyya?; *d* law samaHt, il-matHaf il-waTani ba9iid min il-fundu'?

Go straight on and at the end of the street turn right. Take the second left. The Umayyad Mosque is opposite the market.

6 *a* HaDirtak b-titkallam ingliizi?; *b* shuu shuglak?; *c* inta min dimashq?; *d* inta mitzawwij?; *e* kam sana 9andak?; *f* b-tHibb il-akl il-ingliizi?

7
- shuu b-tishrab?
- law samaHti, biddi waaHid shaay bi na9na9 wa waaHid 9aSiir rumaan.
- il-Hisaab, min faDlik.

You'd get 40 lira change.

8 *1* b-yimshi; *2* b-taakhud; *3* ruuHa raj9a, daraja taanya.

9
- laa' shukran, biddi ashuuf bass.
- aywa, iS-SaHn Hilu bass 9andi SuHuun kitiir.
- mumkin ashuuf ibrii' il-ahwa?
- 'addaysh haada?
- laa', haada ghaali kitiir. mish mumkin!
- miitayn lira mniiH?
- aasif, haada kitiir!

10 ismi Tareq. ana min bayruut. ana muHaasib fi dimashq. ismi Sophie. ana min Edinburgh. ana mudarrisa.

11 *Sophie:* mutabbal, falaafil, samak mashwi, umm 9ali;

Tareq: fuul, mashwi mishakkal, ba'laawa; *Bilal:* mujaddara, kufta mashwiyya, ruzz bi Haliib; *You:* tabbuuleh, dajaaj mashwi, krim karamil.

law samaHti, biddi SalSat TaHiina wa kamaan khubz, min faDlik.

12
- mumkin **taakhudni** lil-maTaar, law samaHt?
- itfaDDal.
- 'addaysh **b-yaakhud** min hawn lil-maTaar?
- ta'riiban **saa9a** waaHda. wayn raayiH HaDirtak?
- ana **raayiH** li London.
- kiif kaanat dimashq?
- **kaanat** mumtaaza. dimashq madiina **jamiila**.
- aymta **ir-riHla**?
- **ba9d** saa9atayn.
- in-shaa' allaah b-nuSal il-maTaar 9al-wa't!
- **in-shaa' allaah**.

grammar

G1 All Arabic **nouns** are either masculine or feminine. Nouns referring to people have the same gender (i.e. masculine or feminine) as the sex of the person. Nouns ending in **-a** are almost always feminine. Similarly most but not all nouns not ending in **-a** are masculine.

The gender of a noun affects adjectives and verbs, which must agree with (that is 'match') the noun in terms of taking a masculine or feminine form. (G7 adjectives; G9–G11 verbs)

G2 Unlike English, Arabic does not add **-s** for the **plural**.

Masculine nouns denoting professions and nationalities add **-iin** to the singular:

maSri- maSriyiin	lubaani- lubnaaniyiin	mudarris- mudarrisiin	muhundis- muhandisiin	muHaasib- muHaasibiin
Egyptian(s)	*Lebanese*	*teacher(s)*	*engineer(s)*	*accountant(s)*

The feminine versions add **-aat** to the singular. This is also how you form the plural of other nouns that end in **-a**, as well as a few that don't:

maSriyya- maSriyyaat	lubnaaniyya- lubaaniyyaat	mudarrisa- mudarrisaat	maHaTTa- maHaTTaat	tilifawn- tilifawnaat
Egyptian(s)	*Lebanese*	*teacher(s)*	*station(s)*	*telephone*

It tends to be easier to learn the plural of all other nouns individually, although there are a number of patterns:

bayt-buyuut *house(s)*   **SaHn-SuHuun** *dish(es)*
SaaHib-aSHaab *friend(s)*   **walad-awlaad** *boys(s)*
fustaan-fasaatiin *dress(es)*   **finjaan-fanaajiin** *cup(s)*
maktab-makaatib *office(s)*   **madrasa-madaaris** *school(s)*
saakin-sukkaan *resident(s)*   **Taalib-Tullaab** *student(s)*

G3 A/an, the

Arabic has no equivalent of the English *a/an*: **bayt** means *house* or *a house*.

The is **il**, which changes according to whether the noun starts with a sun or a moon letter (see list on page 16). Nouns which start with a moon letter keep **il**: **il-bayt** *the house*, **il-maktab** *the office*; nouns which start with a sun letter replace the **l** in **il** by that letter: **is-sayyaara** *the car*, **iT-Taawila** *the table*.

G4 This/that

This/that is **haada** (masculine) and **haadi** (feminine). *These/those* is **hadawl**:
haada Ahmad. *This is Ahmad*; **haadi Maryam.** *This is Miriam.*
hadawl mudarrisiin. *These are teachers.*

In sentences like *This book is expensive*, you have to include the definite article **il**, which changes to **l** in the singular only:
haada-l kitaab ghaali. *This book is expensive*; **haadi-l madiina jamiila.** *This city is beautiful*; **hadawl iT-Tullaab fransiyiin.** *These students are French.*

G5 Possession is expressed by adding an ending onto a noun rather than by using a separate word like *my*, *your*, *their* etc.:

-i *my*	-ak *your* (m)	-ik *your* (f)	-u *his*
-ha *her*	-na *our*	-kum *your* (pl)	-hum *their*

bayt *house*: **bayti** *my house*; **baytu** *his house*
ism *name*: **ismak** *your (m) name*; **ismha** *her name*

If a noun ends in **-a**, this is replaced by **-t** before adding the possessive ending: **madrasa** *school*, **madrasti** *my school*
sayyaara *car*, **sayyaartik** *your (to f) car*

G6 Arabic has no equivalent of the English *'s* for possession. *A manager's office* is simply **maktab mudiir**, or lit. *office manager*. *The manager's office* is **maktab il-mudiir**, with **il** going with the second noun rather than the first; lit. *office the manager*.

If the first noun ends in **-a**, then **-t** is usually added:
sayyaarat mudiir *a manager's car*, **sayyaarat il-mudiir** *the manager's car*

This construction is known in Arabic as the Idaafa.

G7 Adjectives in Arabic normally come after what they describe. They agree in gender (masculine or feminine) and number (singular or plural) with the noun they describe.

If the noun is feminine singular, then the adjective has **-a** at the end:

masculine sing. **bayt jadiid** *a new house*   **maktab kibiir** *a big office*
feminine sing.   **sayyaara jadiida** *a new car*   **madrasa kibiira** *a big school*

All plural nouns which refer to things rather than people behave as feminine singular:

buyuut jadiida *new houses*   **makaatib kibiira** *big offices*

For people, the plural ending of the adjective is often the same as the ending used for nouns denoting professions and nationalities (G2):

awlaad maSriyiin *Egyptian boys*   **banaat maSriyaat** *Egyptian girls*

If a noun is used with **il** *the*, then the adjective also takes **il**:

il-bayt il-abyaD *the White House*, **is-sayyaara il-jadiida** *the new car*

Without **il** in front of the adjective, these would mean *The house is white*, *The car is new*. (G15 'to be'; page 71 comparatives and superlatives)

G8 Personal pronouns, *I, you, he, she, it* etc. are not generally needed with verbs except for emphasis. They're used most often when there's no verb in the sentence, and in particular when English uses *am, is, are* which have no equivalent in Arabic:

ana min ingilterra. *I am from England*; **huwwa mudarris.** *He is a teacher.*

ana	*I/I am*	**iHna**	*we/we are*
inta/inti	*you/you are* (m/f)	**intu**	*you/you are* (pl)
huwwa	*he/he is*	**hum**	*they/they are*
hiyya	*she/she is*		

Verbs

G9 Arabic has two main tenses: the present and the past. There is no equivalent of the infinitive e.g. *to drink*. Verbs are normally listed in the third person masculine (*he*) of the past and present tense. The verb *to drink* is presented as **sharib/yishrab** *he drank/he drinks*.

G10 The **present tense** is formed by placing a prefix onto the front of the verb stem. You find the stem by removing the prefix from the masculine singular (**huwwa**). This prefix is a **y** followed by a helping vowel (usually **i**).

	drink	*go*	*see*	*speak*
ana	ashrab	aruuH	ashuuf	atkallam
inta	tishrab	tiruuH	tishuuf	titkallam
inti	tishrabi	tiruuHi	tishuufi	titkallami
huwwa	yishrab	yiruuH	yishuuf	yitkallam
hiyya	tishrab	tiruuH	tishuuf	titkallam
iHna	nishrab	niruuH	nishuuf	nitkallam
intu	tishrabu	tiruuHu	tishuufu	titkallamu
hum	yishrabu	yiruuHu	yishuufu	yitkallamu

(handwritten margin notes: "(nehny →" "nahnu" "(intum")

In addition to the prefix, the feminine singular *you* adds the ending -**i**, while the feminine plural *you* and *they* both add -**u**.

In some dialects, including Levantine, an extra **b-** is added at the beginning of the verb. Its use differs slightly from region to region but it always denotes a present tense:
b-ashrab shaay kull yawm. *I drink tea every day.*
b-tishrabi 'ahwa? *Do you* (f) *drink coffee?*

This **b-** prefix is not used with **laazim** *must* and **mumkin** *can* (G17):
mumkin titkallam shway shway? *Can you speak more slowly?*

There's no equivalent of the infinitive (the 'to' form of the verb) in Arabic. Instead, the corresponding form of the present tense is used:
biddi aruuH *I want to go*, lit. *I want I go*
biddu yiruuH *He wants to go*, lit. *he wants he goes*

G11 Unlike the present tense, the **past tense** adds a suffix onto the end of the stem. Verbs are grouped, depending on how the spelling of their stem changes, into Sound, Hollow/Middle Weak, Final Weak and Doubled. The majority of verbs in Arabic are in the Sound group.

Verb type	Sound	Hollow	Final weak	Doubled
	booked	*was/were*	*walked*	*liked*
ana	Hajaz<u>t</u>	kun<u>t</u>	mash<u>ayt</u>	Habb<u>ayt</u>
inta	Hajaz<u>t</u>	kun<u>t</u>	mashay<u>t</u>	Habb<u>ayt</u>
inti	Hajaz<u>ti</u>	kun<u>ti</u>	mashay<u>ti</u>	Habb<u>ayti</u>
huwwa	Hajaz	kaan	masha	Habb
hiyya	Hajaz<u>at</u>	kaan<u>at</u>	mash<u>at</u>	Habb<u>at</u>
iHna	Hajaz<u>na</u>	kun<u>na</u>	mashay<u>na</u>	Habb<u>ayna</u>
intu	Hajaz<u>tu</u>	kun<u>tu</u>	mashay<u>tu</u>	Habb<u>aytu</u>
hum	Hajaz<u>u</u>	kaan<u>u</u>	mash<u>u</u>	Habb<u>u</u>

12 Spoken Arabic often uses **active participles** instead of a verb. They have three forms: masculine singular (*I, you, he*), feminine singular (*I, you, she*) and plural (*we, you, they*).

They often indicate that an action is currently going on, rather like the English *-ing* ending (e.g. *I am learning Arabic*):

saakin *I'm/you're/he's living*	**raayiH** *I'm/you're/he's going*
saakna *I'm/you're/she's living*	**raayHa** *I'm/you're/she's going*
saakniin *we/you/they're living*	**raayHiin** *we/you/they're going*

wayn saakin? *Where are you living?/Where do you live?*
wayn raayiH bukra? *Where are you going tomorrow?*

13 **Passive participles** describe the state something is in: *open, closed, booked, broken*. They behave like adjectives and agree with the noun: **il-bank maftuuH.** *The bank (m) is open*; **il-madrasa maftuuHa.** *The school (f) is open.*

14 The **imperative** is the form of the verb used to give instructions or advice: <u>turn</u> *right*, <u>sit</u> *down*, <u>take</u> *two pills with water*. It has three endings depending on whether you're addressing a man, a woman or a group of people. Imperatives are formed by removing any prefix from the present stem and adding the following endings:

<u>b-yi</u>shuuf *he sees, he looks*	**shuuf!** *look* (to m)
	shuuf<u>i</u>! *look* (to f)
	shuuf<u>u</u>! *look* (to pl)

Sometimes **-i** is added to help with pronunciation:
<u>b</u>-yishrab *he drinks*   ishrab! *drink* (to m)

G15 There's no verb **to be**; spoken Arabic does not use *am, are, is*. The presence of the verb *to be* is assumed if there's nothing else acting as a verb in the sentence:
il-akl laziiz. *The food is delicious.* Lit. *the food delicious.*

But you do need the words for *was/were* when talking about the past:
il-akl <u>kaan</u> laziiz *the food <u>was</u> delicious*

fiih means both *there is* and *there are*:
fiih mayya. *There is water*; fiih buyuut. *There are houses.*

G16 There's no verb **to have**. Instead possessive endings (G5) are added to **9and**.

9andi *I have* **9andak/9andik** *you have* (m/f) **9andu/9andha** *he/she has*
9andi bayt fi bayruut. *I have a house in Beirut.*

bidd *to want/need* works in the same way:
biddi *I want/I'd like*   **biddak/biddik** *you want/you'd like* (m/f)

G17 **mumkin** can and **laazim** must don't change to agree with the person, but the verb that follows them does (G10):
mumkin ashuuf? *Can I see?*
laazim tishuuf iT-Tabiib. *You must see the doctor.*

G18 Negatives. There are two negative words: **maa** and **mish**.
maa negates verbs as well as *have, want, there is/there are*:
maa b-atkallam 9arabi. *I don't speak Arabic.*
maa 9andi bayt fi bayruut. *I don't have a house in Beirut.*
maa biddi ashrab shaay. *I don't want to drink tea.*
maa fiih maTaa9im hawn. *There aren't any restaurants around here.*

mish negates active and passive participles, adjectives and sentences without a verb:
binti <u>mish</u> saakna fi Edinburgh. *My daughter doesn't live in Edinburgh.*
il-bank <u>mish</u> maftuuH il-yawm. *The bank isn't open today.*
bayti <u>mish</u> kibiir. *My house isn't big.*
ana <u>mish</u> muhandis. *I'm not an engineer.*

G19 Object pronouns, e.g. *it, him, them* are attached to the end of the verb. The ending you use depends on the gender of the noun it is replacing:
mumkin ashuuf<u>ha</u>? *Can I see her/it* (f)*/them (things)?*
mumkin taakhd<u>u</u>? *Can you take him/it* (m)*?*

Numbers (pp 21, 31, 41, 60, 62) follow varying rules when with a noun:

- **waaHid** *1* usually comes after what it refers to and has a feminine as well as masculine form: **ibn waaHid** *one son*; **bint waaHda** *one daughter*.

- **itnayn** *2* is rarely used when referring to two items (apart from when ordering food and drinks). Instead, the suffix **-ayn** is added to the singular of the noun: **baytayn** *two houses*; **yawmayn** *two days*. If the word ends in **-a** then the suffix is **-tayn**: **sanatayn** *two years*; **sayyaaratayn** *two cars*. This structure is known as the dual in Arabic.

- Numbers 3-10 go before the noun, which is in the plural. The numbers lose their **-a**: **arba9a kutub** *four books*; **khams fanaajiin** *five cups*.

- Numbers over 10 go before the noun, which is in the singular: **9ishriin kitaab** *twenty books*; **arba9iin yawm** *forty days*.

- Numbers 11-19 add **-ar** before the noun: **Hidaashar kitaab** *eleven books*; **khamastaashar Taalib** *fifteen students*.

- With *how many*, the noun is in the singular: **kam sana 9andak/ik?** *How old are you?* lit. *How many year do you have?*

The main exception to the above rules is when ordering items of food and drink, when the numbers are in their countable form and the noun is in the singular. For example:
itnayn 'ahwa *two coffees*; **talaata shaay** *three teas*

Arabic has a root system, with the majority of words made up of three root letters or radicals in the same order. Once you know the combination of radicals for a particular concept then you can build your vocabulary relating to this concept. For example, the radicals **k - t - b** denote the concept of writing:

kitaab *book;* **kutub** *books* **kaatib** *writer;* **kuttaab** *writers*
katabt *I wrote;* **b-aktub** *I write* **maktab** *office;* **makaatib** *offices*
maktaba *library;* **maktabaat** *libraries* **maktuub** *written, letter*

Arabic–English glossary

This glossary contains the words found in this book, with their meanings in the context used here. Verbs are given without the **b-** prefix. Abbreviations: (m) masculine, (f) feminine, (s) singular, (pl) plural.

9

9afwan you're welcome
9ala Tuul straight ahead
9alaykum on/upon you
9al wa't on time
9al-yamiin on the right
9al-yasaar on the left
9andak/9andik you have (m/f)
9andi I have
9ammaan Amman
9andu/9andha he has/ she has
9arabi Arabic; Arab (m)
9ashaanak/9ashaanik for you (m/f)
9ashaani for me
9aSiir juice
9ilba/9ilab can (s/pl)

A

a9raf I know
aakhdu/aakhudha I'll take it/them (m/f)
aakhir end, last (*final*)
aakul I eat
aanisa Miss, waitress
aasif/asfa I'm sorry (m/f)
ab father
abadan never
abyaD/bayDa white (m/f)
adfa9 I pay
aghla more/most expensive
aHibb I like
aHjiz I book
ahlan hi, hello
ahlan fiik/ahlan fiiki *reply* hello (to m/f)

ahlan wa sahlan hello, welcome
aHmar/Hamra red (m/f)
aHsan better, best
akbar bigger, biggest; larger, largest
akhalli I leave (*something*)
akhDar/khaDra green (m/f)
akh/ikhwa brother (s/pl)
akiid certainly
a'iisu/a'iisha I try it on (m/f)
akl food
allaah yisalmak/yisalmik *reply* goodbye (to m/f) *lit.* may God bless you
alwaan/lawn colours (pl/s)
amriika America
amriiki/amriikiyya American (m/f)
ana I/I am
ana faahim/ana fahma I understand (m/f)
ana mish I'm not
anzil I stay
a'rab nearer, nearest
arkhaS cheaper, cheapest
aruuH I go
aSfar/Safra yellow (m/f)
aSghar smaller
ashtiri I buy
ashuufak/ashuufik I see you (to m/f)
asinsiir/aninsiiraat lift (s/pl)
asta9mil I use

aswad/sawda black (m/f)
atkallam I speak
aTwal taller
aw or
awlaad/walad children (pl/s)
awwal first
aymta when?
aywa yes
ayy khidma? Can I help you?
ayy naw9? What/Which kind of?
ayy saa9a What time?
azra'/zar'a (m/f) blue

B

ba9d after, past, beyond
ba9dayn later, afterwards
ba9iid/ba9iida far (m/f)
ba'aal grocer's
baab/abwaab door, gate (s/pl)
baaS/baaSaat bus (s/pl)
baghdaad Baghdad
ba9albak Baalbek
ba'laawa baklava
balad/buldaan country (s/pl)
banaat daughters
bank/bunuuk bank (s/pl)
bass but
bayDa/abyaD white (f/m)
bayruut Beirut
bayt/buyuut house (s/pl)
betinjaan maHshi stuffed aubergines

bi with *things*
biddak/biddik you want? (to m/f)
biddi I want/I would like
biddi ashtiri I want to buy
biddi ashuuf I want to look
biduun without
biira beer
bi-khayr well
bint/banaat daughter (s/pl)
biZ-ZabT exactly
bluuza/bluuzaat blouse (s/pl)
briiTaanya Britain
briiTaani/briiTaaniyya British (m/f)
b-titkallam/b-titkallami you speak (to m/f)
bukra tomorrow
burtu'aan orange
bukra tomorrow

D

da'ii'a/da'aayi' minute (s/pl)
dajaaj chicken
daraja taanya second class
daraja uula first class
dawli international
dhahaab departures
dimashq Damascus
dinaar *currency in Algeria, Bahrain, Iraq, Jordan, Kuwait, Libya and Tunisia*
dirham *currency in Morocco and UAE*
dukkaan/dakaakiin shop (s/pl)
duktuur/dakaatra doctor (s/pl)

F

faahim/faahma understand (m/f)
faas Fez
fanaajiin/finjaan cups (pl/s)
fawaakih fruit
fi9lan really, indeed
fi aakhir at the end
fi awwal in/on the first
fiih there is/there are
finjaan/fanaajiin cup (s/pl)
fransa France
fransi/fransiyya French (m/f)
fukhaar earthenware
fundu'/fanaadi' hotel (s/pl)
fustaan/fasaatiin dress (s/pl)
fuTuur breakfast
fuul beans

G

garsawn waiter (aanisa waitress)
ghaali/ghaalya expensive (m/f)
ghurfa/ghuraf room (s/pl)
ghurfa raqm room number
gineeh pound *currency*
gineeh isterliini pound Sterling
gineeh maSri Egyptian pound

H

haada/haadi this (m/f)
haada kullu. That's all.
HaaDir OK
Habb il-haal cardamom
hadawl these, those
Hadii'a/Hadaayi' park (s/pl)

HaDirtak/HaDirtik *formal* you (m/f)
Hajz reservation
Hajazt I booked
Hajazt/Hajazti you booked (to m/f)
Halab Aleppo
Haliib milk
Hammaam bathroom
Hammaam is-sibaaHa the swimming pool
Hamra/aHmar red (f/m)
Hawaali about, roughly
hawn here
Hida9sh eleven
Hilu/Hilwa pretty (m/f)
Hilu dessert
Hisaab/Hisaabaat bill (s/pl)
hiyya she/she is
hulanda Holland
hunaak over there
huwwa he/he is

I

ibn/abnaa' son (s/pl)
ibrii' shaay/'ahwa tea/coffee pot
id-daar il-bayDa Casablanca
iftaH/iftaHi open *instruction* (to m/f)
ikhwa/akh brothers (pl/s)
il-Hamdullilaah praise be to God
il-imaaraat The Emirates
il-jadiida Al-Jadida
il-jazaa'ir Algiers, Algeria
il-maghrib Morocco
il-qaahira Cairo
il-urdun Jordan
il-yawm today
ila to, towards
illa except
imbaariH yesterday
ingilterra England

ingliizi/ingliiziyya
English (m/f)
in shaa' allaah God willing
inta *informal* you/you
are (m)
inti *informal* you/you
are (f)
irlanda Ireland
irlandi/irlandiyya Irish
(m/f)
ir-ribaaT Rabat
ir-riyaaD Riyadh
ishaarat il-muruur the
traffic lights
isharb scarf
ish-sharaf ili *reply* the
pleasure is mine
iskandariyya Alexandria
iskutlanda Scotland
iskutlandi/iskutlandiyya
Scottish (m/f)
ism name
ismak your name (to m)
ismi my name
ismik your name (to f)
is-sa9uudiyya Saudi
Arabia
is-salaam 9alaykum
may peace be upon you
istimaara/istimaaraat
form (s/pl)
itfaDDal/itfaDDali here
you are; come this way;
be my guest (to m/f)
iT-Taabi' il-awwal the
first floor

J

jaami9/jawaami9
mosque (s/pl)
jaami9a/jaami9aat
university s/pl)
jaay next
jadda Jeddah
jakayt/jakaytaat jacket
(s/pl)
jamiil/jamiila beautiful
(m/f)

janb near
jariida/jaraa'id
newspaper (s/pl)
jawaaz raqm passport
number
jawaaz safar passport
jawzi my husband
jiddan very
jinsiyya nationality

K

kaan he/it was
kaanat she/it was
kaas/kaasaat glass (s/pl)
kam? How many?
kamaan as well; another
kart/kuruut postcard
(s/pl)
khaDra/akhDar green
(f/m)
khidma service
khubz bread
khud/khudi take
instruction (to m/f)
khuSuuSan especially
kibiir/kibiira big, large
(m/f)
kiif how
kiif il-Haal? How are you?
kilomitr kilometre
kitaab/kutub book (s/pl)
kitiir many, a lot; very
kull every, all, whole
kull yawm every day
kunt I was/you were (m)
kuruut postcards
kushk kiosk
kwayyis good

L

laa' no
laakin but
laazim one must, should
laHma meat
lamuun lemon
laTiif/laTiifa nice (m/f)
lawn/alwaan colour
(s/pl)

law samaHt/law
samaHti excuse me;
please (to m/f)
layla/layaali night (s/pl)
laziiz/laziiza delicious
(m/f)
li to
liff/liffi turn *instruction*
(to m/f)
liibya Libya
lira pound *currency*
lira suuriyya Syrian
pound *currency*
lista menu
lubnaan Lebanon
lubnaani/lubnaaniyya
Lebanese (m/f)

M

ma9a as-salaama
goodbye
maa don't
maa 9andi I don't have
maa b-a9raf I don't know
maa biddi I don't want
ma'aas/ma'aasaat size
(s/pl)
madaam Mrs
madiina/mudun town,
city (s/pl)
madiinti my town, my
city
madrasa/madaaris
school (s/pl)
madrasat il-awlaad the
boys' school
ma'fuul/ma'fuula closed
(m/f)
maftuuH/maftuuHa
open (m/f)
maghribi/maghribiyya
Moroccan (m/f)
maHaTTa/maHaTTaat
station (s/pl)
maHaTTat il-baaSaat
the bus station
maHaTTat il-qiTaar the
train station

maHjuuz booked, reserved
majalla/majallaat magazine (s/pl)
majmuu9 total
makaan il-iqaama the place of residence
maktab/makaatib office (s/pl)
maktab bariid post office
maktab isti9laamaat tourist information office
manga mango
maqha/maqaahi café (s/pl)
maqha internet internet café
marHaba hello
marHabtayn *reply to marHaba lit. two hellos*
marraaksh Marrakesh
marra taanya again, a second time
marti my wife
masaa evening
masaa il-khayr good evening
masaa in-nuur *reply* good evening
mashwiyyaat charcoal-grilled food
masjid/masaajid mosque (s/pl)
maSr Egypt
maSri/maSriyya Egyptian (m/f)
maT9am/maTaa9im restaurant (s/pl)
maTaar/maTaaraat airport (s/pl)
matHaf/mataaHif museum (s/pl)
mayya water
mayya ma9daniyya mineral water
maZbuuT semi-sweet (*for coffee*)

mazza mezze
mi'aabil opposite
min from
min faDlak/faDlik please (to m/f)
min hawn from here
mish not
mish ba9iid/ba9iida It's not far away (m/f)
mish faahim/faahma I don't understand (m/f)
mish mumkin it's not possible
mitzawwij/mitzawwija married (m/f)
mitr metre
mniiH OK
mubayl mobile
mudarris/mudarrisa/ mudarrisiin teacher (m/f/pl)
mudiir/mudiira manager (m/f)
muftaaH/mafaatiiH key (s/pl)
muhandis/muhandisa engineer (m/f)
muHaasib/muHaasiba accountant (m/f)
mumarriD/mumarriDa nurse (m/f)
mumkin it is possible, can
mumkin adfa9? Can I pay?
mumkin a'iisu/a'iisha? Can I try it on? (m/f)
mumkin aruuH? Can I go?
mumkin ashuuf ...? Can I have a look at ...?
mumkin titkallam/ titkallami? Can you speak? (to m/f)
mumtaaz/mumtaaza excellent (m/f)
muqabbilaat starters

mustashfa/ mustashfayaat hospital (s/pl)

N
na9am yes
na9na9 mint
nabaati vegetarian
nuSS half
nuSS saa9a half an hour

Q/'
qiTaar/qiTaaraat train (s/pl)
qunsuliyya consulate
'addaysh how much is/ are
'ahwa coffee
'amiiS/'umSaan shirt (s/pl)
'aniina bottle
'ariib/'ariiba close by (m/f)

R
raayiH/raayHa going (m/f)
raSiif/arSifa platform (s/pl)
riHla/riHlaat journey, trip, flight (s/pl)
rakhiiS cheap
raqm/arqaam number (s/pl)
riHla sa9iida bon voyage
riyaal *currency in Saudi Arabia, Qatar and Oman*
rub9 quarter
rub9 saa9a a quarter of an hour
rumaan pomegranate
ruuH/ruuHi go *instruction* (m/f)
ruuHa single (ticket)
ruuHa raj9a return (ticket)
ruzz rice

S

SaaHib/SaaHiba/aSHaab friend (m/f/pl)
SaaHibi/SaaHibti my friend (m/f)
saakin/saakna am living/lives (m/f)
SabaaH morning
SabaaH il-khayr good morning
SabaaH in-nuur *reply* good morning
Safra/aSfar yellow (f/m)
Saghiir/Saghiira small (m/f)
SaHn/SuHuun large dish (s/pl)
salaaTa/salaaTaat salad (s/pl)
SalSat TaHiina sesame paste
samak fish
sana/siniin year (s/pl)
sawda/aswad black (f/m)
Saydaliyya/saydaliyyaat chemist's (s/pl)
sayyaara/sayyaaraat car (s/pl)
sayyid Mr
shaari9/shawaari9 road, street (s/pl)
shaay tea
shakhS/ashkhaaS person/people
shakhSayn two people
shakhS waaHid one person
shammaam melon
shanTa/shunaT bag (s/pl)
sharika/sharikaat company (s/pl)
shi taani anything else
shughl work, business (noun)
shukran thank you
shuu what
shuuf/shuufi look (to m/f)

shway/shwayya a little, slowly
Siniyya/Sawaani tray (s/pl)
sukkar sugar
suu'/aswaa' market (s/pl)
suubermarket supermarket
Suura/Suwar photograph, picture (s/pl)
suuriya Syria
suuri/suuriyya Syrian (m/f)

T

Taabi9/Tawaabi9 postage stamp (s/pl)
taakhud it takes (f)
taakhudni you take me (to m)
taakul/taakli you eat (m/f)
Taalib/Taaliba/Tullaab student (m/f/pl)
taani/taanya second; other (m/f)
Taawila/Taawilaat table (s/pl)
Tab9an certainly, of course
Tabiib/Tabiiba/aTibbaa' doctor (m/f/pl)
taksi/taksiyaat taxi (s/pl)
takyiif air-conditioning
taman/atmaan price (s/pl)
Tanja Tangiers
Taraablus Tripoli
ta'riiban almost, roughly
tasharrafna pleased to meet you
tawaabil spices
Tawiil tall
Tayyib fine, OK
tazkara/tazaakir ticket (s/pl)

tazkara ruuHa single ticket
tazkara ruuHa raj9a return ticket
tazkartayn two tickets
tHibb/tHibbi? would you like? (m/f)
tilifawn/tilifawnaat telephone (s/pl)
tinzil/tinzili you stay (to m/f)
tishrab/tishrabi you (m/f) drink
ti'uul li/ti'uuli li tell me/say to me (to m/f)
tuffaaH apple
Tullaab/Taalib students (pl/s)
tult a third
tuTlub/tuTlubi you order (m/f)
tuunis Tunisia, Tunis
tuunisi/tuunisiyya Tunisian (m/f)

U

ukht/ikhwaat sister (s/pl)
umm/ummahaat mother (s/pl)
urduni/urduniyya Jordanian (m/f)
ustaaz/ustaaza lecturer (m/f)
utiil/utiilaat hotel (s/pl)

W

wa and
wa 9alaykum is-salaam and upon you be peace
waaHid/waaHda one (m/f)
walad/awlaad child/children
waraa behind
waTani national
wasT centre, middle
wayn where
wi and

w-inta/w-inti? and you?
(to m/f)
wuSuul arrivals

Y

ya *before a person's name*
yaakhud it takes (m)
ya9ni I/you mean
yamiin right
yasaar left
yawm day

yi'fil/ti'fil it closes (m/f)
yiftaH/tiftaH it opens
(m/f)
yimshi it departs (m)
yishrab he drinks
yuSal it arrives (m)

Z

zamiil/zamiila colleague
(m/f)

zamiili/zamiilti my
colleague (m/f)
zar'a/azra' blue (f/m)
ziyaada extra

English–Arabic glossary

A

about Hawaali
accountant muHaasib/
muHaasiba (m/f)
after ba9d
afterwards ba9dayn
again marra taanya
air-conditioning takyiif
airport maTaar/
maTaaraat (s/pl)
Aleppo Halab
Alexandria iskandariyya
Algiers, Algeria il-jazaa'ir
Al-Jadida il-jadiida
all kull
almost ta'riiban
America amriika
American amriiki/
amriikiyya (m/f)
Amman 9ammaan
and wa/wi
and you? w-inta/w-inti?
(to m/f)
another kamaan
anything else shi taani
apple tuffaaH
Arabic; Arab 9arabi (m)
arrivals wuSuul
arrive: it arrives
yuSal (m)
as well kamaan
aubergines (stuffed)
betinjaan maHshi

B

Baalbek ba9albak
bag shanTa/shunaT (s/pl)
Baghdad baghdaad
baklava ba'laawa
bank bank/bunuuk (s/pl)
bathroom Hammaam
be able: it is possible, can
mumkin
be: I was/you were
kunt (m)

beans fuul
beautiful jamiil/jamiila
(m/f)
beer biira
behind waraa
Beirut bayruut
best aHsan
better aHsan
beyond ba9d
big kibiir/kibiira (m/f)
bigger, biggest akbar
bill Hisaab/
Hisaabaat (s/pl)
black aswad/sawda (m/f)
blouse bluuza/
bluuzaat (s/pl)
blue azra'/zar'a (m/f)
bon voyage riHla sa9iida
book kitaab/kutub (s/pl)
book: I book aHjiz
book: I booked Hajazt
booked: you booked
Hajazt/Hajazti (to m/f)
bottle 'aniina
bread khubz
breakfast fuTuur
Britain briiTaanya
British briiTaani/
briiTaaniyya (m/f)
brother akh/ikhwa (s/pl)
bus baaS/baaSaat (s/pl)
bus station maHaTTat
il-baaSaat
business (occupation)
shughl
but bass; laakin
buy: I buy ashtiri; I want
to buy biddi ashtiri

C

café maqha/
maqaahi (s/pl)
Cairo il-qaahira
can (metal container)
9ilba/9ilab (s/pl)

car sayyaara/
sayyaaraat (s/pl)
cardamom Habb il-haal
Casablanca id-daar
il-bayDa
centre wasT
certainly akiid
cheap rakhiiS
cheaper, cheapest arkhaS
chemist's Saydaliyya/
Saydaliyyaat (s/pl)
chicken dajaaj
child/children walad/
awlaad (s/pl)
city madiina/mudun
(s/pl); my city madiinti
close by 'ariib/
'ariiba (m/f)
close: it closes yi'fil/
ti'fil (m/f)
closed ma'fuul/
ma'fuula (m/f)
coffee 'ahwa
coffee pot ibrii' 'ahwa
colleague zamiil/zamiila
(m/f); my colleague
zamiili/zamiilti (m/f)
colour lawn/alwaan (s/pl)
come this way itfaDDal/
itfaDDali (to m/f)
company sharika/
sharikaat (s/pl)
consulate qunsuliyya
country balad/
buldaan (s/pl)
cup finjaan/
fanaajiin (s/pl)

D

Damascus dimashq
daughter bint/
banaat (s/pl)
day yawm; every day kull
yawm
delicious laziiz/laziiza
(m/f)

depart: it departs yimshi (m)

departures dhahaab

dessert Hilu

dish: large dish SaHn/ SuHuun (s/pl)

doctor (medical) Tabiib/ Tabiiba/aTibbaa' (m/f/ pl); (title) duktuur/ dakaatra (s/pl)

don't maa

door baab/abwaab (s/pl)

dress fustaan/ fasaatiin (s/pl)

drink: you drink tishrab/ tishrabi (m/f)

drinks: he drinks yishrab

E

earthenware fukhaar

eat: I eat aakul

eat: you eat taakul/ taakli (m/f)

Egypt maSr

Egyptian maSri/ maSriyya (m/f)

Egyptian pound gineeh maSri

eleven Hida9sh

end (final) aakhir; at the end fi aakhir

engineer muhandis/ muhandisa (m/f)

England ingilterra

English ingliizi/ ingliiziyya (m/f)

especially khuSuuSan

evening masaa

every kull; every day kull yawm

exactly biZ-ZabT

excellent mumtaaz/ mumtaaza (m/f)

except illa

excuse me law samaHt/ law samaHti (to m/f)

expensive ghaali/ ghaalya (m/f); more/

most expensive aghla

extra ziyaada

F

far ba9iid/ba9iida (m/f); It's not far away mish ba9iid/ba9iida (m/f)

father ab

Fez faas

fine Tayyib

first awwal; in/on the first fi awwal

first class daraja uula

fish samak

flight riHla/riHlaat (s/pl)

floor: first floor iT-Taabi' il-awwal

food akl

form istimaara/ istimaaraat (s/pl)

France fransa

French fransi/ fransiyya (m/f)

friend SaaHib/SaaHiba/ aSHaab (m/f/pl); my friend SaaHibi/ SaaHibti (m/f)

from min; from here min hawn

fruit fawaakih

G

gate baab/abwaab (s/pl)

glass kaas/kaasaat (s/pl)

go (instruction) ruuH/ ruuHi (m/f)

go: I go aruuH; Can I go? mumkin aruuH?

God willing in shaa' allaah

going raayiH/ raayHa (m/f)

good kwayyis

good evening masaa il-khayr; (reply) masaa in-nuur

good morning SabaaH il-khayr; (reply) SabaaH in-nuur

goodbye ma9a as-salaama; (reply) allaah yisalmak/yisalmik (to m/f)

green akhDar/ khaDra (m/f)

grilled food (charcoal) mashwiyyaat

grocer's ba'aal

H

half nuSS; half an hour nuSS saa9a

has: he has/she has 9andu/9andha (m/f)

have: I have 9andi; I don't have maa 9andi

have: you have 9andak/9andik (m/f)

he/he is huwwa

he/it was kaan

hello (formal) marHaba; (reply) marHabtayn

hello (informal) ahlan; (reply) ahlan fiik/ahlan fiiki (to m/f)

hello, welcome ahlan wa sahlan

help: Can I help you? ayy khidma?

here hawn

here you are itfaDDal/ itfaDDali (to m/f)

hi ahlan; (reply) ahlan fiik/ahlan fiiki (to m/f)

Holland hulanda

hospital mustashfa/ mustashfayaat (s/pl)

hotel fundu'/fanaadi' (s/pl); utiil/utiilaat (s/pl)

house bayt/buyuut (s/pl)

how kiif

How are you? kiif il-Haal?

How many? kam?

how much is/are 'addaysh

husband: my husband jawzi

I

I ana

I am ana; I'm not ana mish

indeed fi9lan

international dawli

internet café maqha

internet

Ireland irlanda

Irish irlandi/ irlandiyya (m/f)

J

jacket jakayt/jakaytaat (s/pl)

Jeddah jadda

Jordan il-urdun

Jordanian urduni/ urduniyya (m/f)

journey riHla/riHlaat (s/pl)

juice 9aSiir

K

key muftaaH/mafaatiiH (s/pl)

kilometre kilomitr

kiosk kushk

know: I know a9raf; I don't know maa b-a9raf

L

large kibiir/kibiira (m/f)

larger, largest akbar

last (final) aakhir

later ba9dayn

leave: I leave (something) akhalli

Lebanese lubnaani/ lubnaaniyya (m/f)

Lebanon lubnaan

lecturer ustaaz/ ustaaza (m/f)

left yasaar; on the left 9al-yasaar

lemon lamuun

Libya liibya

lift asinsiir/

aninsiiraat (s/pl)

like: I like aHibb

like: would you like? tHibb/tHibbi? (m/f)

little: a little shway/ shwayya

live/am living saakin/ saakna (m/f)

look shuuf/shuufi (to m/f)

look: Can I have a look at ...? mumkin ashuuf ...?

look: I want to look biddi ashuuf

lot: a lot kitiir

M

magazine majalla/ majallaat (s/pl)

manager mudiir/mudiira (m/f)

mango manga

many kitiir

many: How many? kam?

market suu'/aswaa' (s/pl)

Marrakesh marraaksh

married mitzawwij/ mitzawwija (m/f)

me: for me 9ashaani

mean: I/you mean ya9ni

meat laHma

melon shammaam

menu lista

metre mitr

mezze mazza

middle wasT

milk Haliib

mineral water mayya ma9daniyya

mint na9na9

minute da'ii'a/ da'aayi' (s/pl)

Miss aanisa

mobile mubayl

morning SabaaH

Moroccan maghribi/ maghribiyya (m/f)

Morocco il-maghrib

mosque jaami9/ jawaami9 (s/pl); masjid/ masaajid (s/pl)

mother umm/ ummahaat (s/pl)

Mr sayyid

Mrs madaam

much: how much is/are 'addaysh

museum matHaf/ mataaHif (s/pl)

must: one must, should laazim

N

name ism; my name is ... ismi ...

name: your name ismak/ ismik (to m/f)

national waTani

nationality jinsiyya

near janb

nearer, nearest a'rab

never abadan

newspaper jariida/ jaraa'id (s/pl)

next jay

nice laTiif/laTiifa (m/f)

night layla/layaali (s/pl)

no laa'

not mish

number raqm/ arqaam (s/pl)

nurse mumarriD/ mumarriDa (m/f)

O

of course Tab9an

office maktab/ makaatib (s/pl)

OK HaaDir; mniiH; Tayyib

one waaHid/ waaHda (m/f)

open maftuuH/ maftuuHa (m/f)

open (instruction) iftaH/
iftaHi (to m/f)
open: it opens yiftaH/
tiftaH (m/f)
opposite mi'aabil
or aw
orange burtu'aan
order: you order tuTlub/
tuTlubi (m/f)
other taani/taanya (m/f)
over there hunaak

P

park Hadii'a/Hadaayi'
(s/pl)
passport jawaaz safar
passport number jawaaz
raqm
past ba9d
pay: I pay adfa9; Can I
pay? mumkin adfa9?
peace: and upon you
be peace wa 9alaykum
is-salaam; (reply)
is-salaam 9alaykum
people: two people
shakhSayn
person/people shakhS/
ashkhaaS (s/pl)
person: one person
shakhS waaHid
photograph Suura/
Suwar (s/pl)
picture Suura/Suwar (s/pl)
platform raSiif/
arSifa (s/pl)
please min faDlak/faDlik
(to m/f); law samaHt/
law samaHti (to m/f);
pleased to meet you
tasharrafna; (reply) ish-
sharaf ili
pomegranate rumaan
possible: it is possible
mumkin; it's not possible
mish mumkin
post office maktab bariid
postage stamp Taabi9/

Tawaabi9 (s/pl)
postcard kart/kuruut
(s/pl)
pound (currency) gineeh
(Egyptian); lira (Syrian)
pound Sterling gineeh
isterliini
praise be to God
il-Hamdullilaah
pretty Hilu/Hilwa (m/f)
price taman/atmaan
(s/pl)

Q

quarter rub9; a quarter
of an hour rub9 saa9a

R

Rabat ir-ribaaT
really fi9lan
red aHmar/Hamra (m/f)
reservation Hajz
reserved maHjuuz
residence makaan
il-iqaama
restaurant maT9am/
maTaa9im (s/pl)
return ruuHa raj9a;
return ticket tazkara
ruuHa raj9a
rice ruzz
right yamiin; on the
right 9al-yamiin Riyadh
ir-riyaaD
road shaari9/shawaari9
(s/pl)
room ghurfa/ghuraf (s/pl)
room number ghurfa
raqm
roughly Hawaali; ta'riiban

S

salad salaaTa/
salaaTaat (s/pl)
Saudi Arabia is-sa9uudiyya
scarf isharb
school madrasa/
madaaris (s/pl)

school: boys' school
madrasat il-awlaad
Scotland iskutlanda
Scottish iskutlandi/
iskutlandiyya (m/f)
second taani/taanya
(m/f)
second class daraja
taanya
second: a second time
marra taanya
see: I see you ashuufak/
ashuufik (to m/f)
semi-sweet (for coffee)
maZbuuT
service khidma
sesame paste SalSat
TaHiina
she/it was kaanat
she/she is hiyya
shirt 'amiiS/
'umSaan (s/pl)
shop dukkaan/
dakaakiin (s/pl)
should: one should
laazim
single ruuHa; single
ticket tazkara ruuHa
sister ukht/ikhwaat (s/pl)
size ma'aas/
ma'aasaat (s/pl)
slowly shway/shwayya
small Saghiir/
Saghiira (m/f)
smaller aSghar
son ibn/abnaa' (s/pl)
sorry: I'm sorry aasif/
asfa (m/f)
speak: Can you speak?
mumkin titkallam/
titkallami? (to m/f)
speak: I speak atkallam
speak: you speak
b-titkallam/b-titkallami
(to m/f)
spices tawaabil
starters muqabbilaat
station maHaTTa/
maHaTTaat (s/pl)

stay: I stay anzil
stay: you stay tinzil/
tinzili (to m/f)
straight ahead 9ala Tuul
street shaari9/
shawaari9 (s/pl)
student Taalib/Taaliba/
Tullaab (m/f/pl)
sugar sukkar
supermarket
suubermarket
swimming pool
Hammaam is-sibaaHa
Syria suuriya
Syrian suuri/
suuriyya (m/f)
Syrian currency (pound)
lira suuriyya

T

table Taawila/Taawilaat
(s/pl)
take (instruction) khud/
khudi (to m/f)
take: I'll take it/them
aakhdu/aakhudha
take: it takes yaakhud/
taakhud (m/f)
take: you take me
taakhudni (to m)
tall Tawiil
taller aTwal
Tangiers Tanja
taxi taksi/taksiyaat (s/pl)
tea shaay
tea pot ibrii' shaay
teacher mudarris/
mudarrisa/mudarrisiin
(m/f/pl)
telephone tilifawn/
tilifawnaat (s/pl)
tell me/say to me ti'uul
li/ti'uuli li (to m/f)
thank you shukran
That's all. haada kullu.
The Emirates il-imaaraat
there is/there are fiih
these hadawl

third: a third tult
this haada/haadi (m/f)
those hadawl
ticket tazkara/tazaakir
(s/pl); two tickets
tazkartayn
time: on time 9al wa't
time: What time? ayy
saa9a
to li
today il-yawm
tomorrow bukra
total majmuu9
tourist information office
maktab isti9laamaat
towards/to ila
town madiina/mudun
(s/pl); my town madiinti
traffic lights ishaarat
il-muruur
train qiTaar/qiTaaraat
(s/pl)
train station maHaTTat
il-qiTaar
tray Siniyya/
Sawaani (s/pl)
trip riHla/riHlaat (s/pl)
Tripoli Taraablus
try: I try it on a'iisu/
a'iisha (m/f); Can I try
it on? mumkin a'iisu/
a'iisha? (m/f)
Tunisia, Tunis tuunis
Tunisian tuunisi/
tuunisiyya (m/f)
turn (instruction) (liff/
liffi (to m/f)

U

understand faahim/
faahma (m/f)
understand: I understand
ana faahim/ana fahma
(m/f); I don't understand
mish faahim/faahma
(m/f)
university jaami9a/

jaami9aat (s/pl)
use: I use asta9mil

V

vegetarian nabaati
very jiddan

W

waiter garsawn
waitress aanisa
want: I want/I would like
biddi; I don't want maa
biddi
want: you want? biddak/
biddik (to m/f)
was: it was kaan
water mayya
welcome, hello ahlan wa
sahlan
welcome: you're
welcome 9afwan
well bi-khayr
what shuu; What kind
of? ayy naw9?
when? aymta
where wayn
white abyaD/
bayDa (m/f)
whole kull
wife: my wife marti
with (things) bi
without biduun
work (occupation) shughl

Y

year sana/siniin (s/pl)
yellow aSfar/Safra (m/f)
yes aywa/na9am
yesterday imbaariH
you (formal) HaDirtak/
HaDirtik (m/f)
you/you are (informal)
inta/inti (m/f); And you?
w-inta/w-inti? (to m/f)
you: for you 9ashaanak/
9ashaanik (m/f)